W9-BNT-520

Published by Doubleday, a division of
Bantam Doubleday Dell Publishing Group, Inc.,
666 Fifth Avenue, New York, New York 10103

Doubleday and the portrayal of an anchor with a
dolphin are trademarks of Doubleday, a division of
Bantam Doubleday Dell Publishing Goup, Inc.

Library of Congress Cataloging-in-Publication Data
The Doubleday children's atlas.
    Includes index.
    Summary: Introduces the people, places, countries, and
continents of the world through relief maps, facts,
figures, and over 100 color photographs.
    1. Atlases. [1. Atlases. 2. Geography] I. Olliver,
Jane. II. Title. III. Title: Children's atlas.
G1021.D6 1987 912 86-675232
ISBN 0-385-23760-X

Copyright © 1987 by Kingfisher, Ltd.
First Edition in United States of America, 1987

Published in the United Kingdom under the
title THE KINGFISHER CHILDREN'S WORLD ATLAS

6 8 9 7 5

THE DOUBLEDAY CHILDREN'S ATLAS

Edited by Jane Olliver

Doubleday

NEW YORK   LONDON   TORONTO   SYDNEY   AUCKLAND

Contents

THE SCALE

Kilometers
0   1000   2000   3000

0   1000   2000
Miles

N

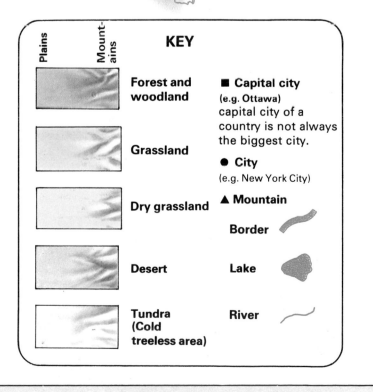

Use the location map to find where a
particular country or region is in the world.

How to Use a Map

Many kinds of maps can be drawn. They give us
different information. A *political* map, like the
one on pages 10–11, shows the boundaries of the
world's countries. The *physical* map on pages 12–
13 shows the land's surface with its oceans, rivers,
lakes, and mountains. Colors and *symbols* are
used on maps to give information. Look at the
map above. To see what the colors and symbols
mean, check the *key* on the right.

Maps are much smaller than the actual area of
the countries they show. But they are always
drawn to *scale*. Scale means the comparison
between the map size and the real size. If the scale
is written like this – 1:800,000, it means that one
inch on the map stands for 800,000 inches (12.5
miles) on the ground. The maps in this atlas have
a bar scale. You can measure any distance on the
map, then compare it to the bar scale to find the
real land distance.

KEY

Plains

Mountains

Forest and woodland

Grassland

Dry grassland

Desert

Tundra (Cold treeless area)

■ **Capital city**
(e.g. Ottawa)
capital city of a
country is not always
the biggest city.

● **City**
(e.g. New York City)

▲ **Mountain**

Border

Lake

River

Maps and Mapmaking

Our earth is one of nine planets circling around the sun. It is the fifth-largest planet in the solar system. The earth is shaped like a ball. But it is slightly flattened at the top and bottom.

We can show the earth's land and seas as they are by drawing a map on the surface of a *globe*. A globe is a round ball, shaped like the earth. You can see a picture of a globe on the right. When it turns, we can see all the sides one by one. Look at these four views of the same globe.

A globe

Western   Eastern   Northern   Southern

But if we want to show all the earth's sides at once on flat paper, we have to draw a *projection*. A projection is a flat drawing of rounded sections of the globe. It is impossible to lay a curved surface flat without twisting and pulling some of the sections. Try drawing a picture on an orange. Then peel the orange in segments and flatten them on a table. You will not be able to do it without squashing the peel out of shape, or *distorting* it. What has happened to your drawing? It is distorted. All maps of the world are distorted in one way or another.

The surface of the globe being peeled off.

The surface of the globe stretched flat.

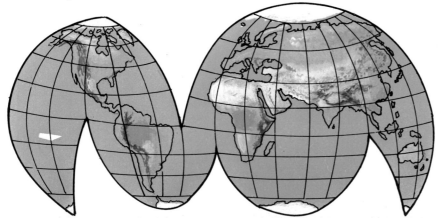

Above and left you can see one method of peeling the surface off a globe to make a flat map. The lines on the map running from north to south are lines of *longitude*. The lines running from east to west are the lines of *latitude*. These lines are very useful. Mapmakers use them to make sure that cities and boundaries are put in the right place on the map.

The Earth:
Facts and Figures

Core

Mantle

Crust

EARTH FACTS

Circumference around the equator: 24,902 miles.

Circumference around the poles: 24,860 miles.

Distance to center of earth: About 3,963.34 miles.

Surface area: About 197,751,000 square miles. Sea covers 71 percent of the surface of the earth.

Average distance from the sun: 93,000,000 miles. The earth is farther away from the sun in July than in January.

Rotation Speed: At the equator, the earth rotates on its axis at 1,032 miles per hour.

Speed in orbit: The earth travels at 18.5 miles per second.

Average distance from moon: 238,860 miles.

HIGHEST MOUNTAINS

	feet
Everest (Himalaya-Nepal/Tibet)	29,028
Godwin Austen (Pakistan/India)	28,250
Kanchenjunga (Himalaya-Nepal/Sikkim)	28,208
Makalu (Himalaya-Nepal/Tibet)	27,824
Dhaulagiri (Himalaya-Nepal)	26,810
Nanga Parbat (Himalaya-India)	26,660
Annapurna (Himalaya-Nepal)	26,504
Communism Peak (U.S.S.R.)	24,590
Aconcagua (Andes-Argentina)	22,831
McKinley (Alaska)	20,320
Kilimanjaro (Tanzania)	19,340
Elbrus (Caucasus-U.S.S.R.)	18,510

The highest mountain is the peak of Everest above Khumbu glacier.

LONGEST RIVERS

	miles
Nile (Africa)	4,145
Amazon (S. America)	3,915
Yangtze (China)	3,910
Mississippi-Missouri-Red Rock (N. America)	3,741
Ob-Irtysh (U.S.S.R.)	3,362
Yenisei (U.S.S.R.)	3,100
Hwang Ho	2,877
Amur (Asia)	2,744
Lena (U.S.S.R.)	2,734
Zaire* (Africa)	2,718
Mackenzie-Peace-Finlay (Canada)	2,635
Mekong (S.E. Asia)	2,610
Niger (Africa)	2,548

*Formerly Congo River

LARGEST ISLANDS

	square miles
Australia	2,968,125
Greenland	840,000
New Guinea	305,000
Borneo	290,000
Madagascar	226,400
Baffin I.	195,928
Sumatra	164,000
Honshu	88,000
Great Britain	84,400
Victoria I.	83,896
Ellesmere	75,767

OCEANS

	square miles
Pacific	61,186,000
Atlantic	31,862,000
Indian	28,350,000
Arctic	5,427,000

The highest waterfall is part of the Angel Falls, Venezuela.

MAJOR WATERFALLS

Highest	feet
Angel Falls (Venezuela)	3,212
Tugela Falls (South Africa)	3,110
Yosemite Falls (California)	2,425

Greatest volume	cubic feet per second
Niagara (N. America)	212,000

DESERTS

	square miles
Sahara	3,243,500
Australian Desert	600,000
Arabian Desert	520,000
Gobi	402,000
Kalahari	200,000

LARGEST LAKES

	square miles
Caspian Sea (U.S.S.R./Iran)	143,243
Superior (U.S.A./Canada)	31,820
Victoria Nyanza (Africa)	26,724
Aral (U.S.S.R.)	25,676
Huron (U.S.A./Canada)	23,010
Michigan (U.S.A.)	22,400
Tanganyika (Africa)	12,650
Baikal (U.S.S.R.)	12,162
Great Bear (Canada)	12,096
Malawi* (Africa)	11,555
Great Slave Lake (Canada)	11,031

*Also called Lake Nyasa

The largest desert is the Sahara, which stretches across northern Africa.

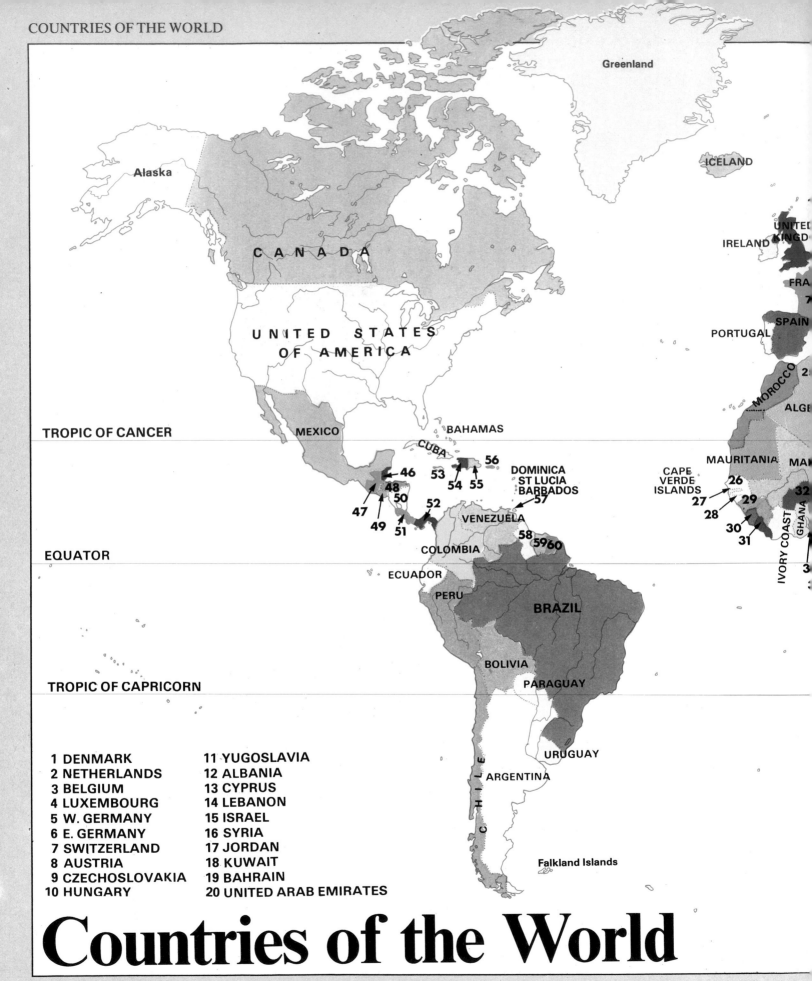

Greenland

ICELAND

Alaska

C A N A D A

UNITED KINGD

IRELAND

FRA
7

UNITED STATES OF AMERICA

PORTUGAL SPAIN

MOROCCO 2

ALGE

TROPIC OF CANCER

MEXICO

BAHAMAS

CUBA

MAURITANIA MA

CAPE VERDE ISLANDS

← 46
53
54 55

56

DOMINICA
ST LUCIA
BARBADOS

26
27
28

32

48
50
52

57

29

47
49 51

VENEZUELA

58 59 60

30
31

EQUATOR

COLOMBIA

IVORY COAST GHANA

3

ECUADOR

PERU

BRAZIL

BOLIVIA

TROPIC OF CAPRICORN

PARAGUAY

URUGUAY

CHILE ARGENTINA

Falkland Islands

1 DENMARK
2 NETHERLANDS
3 BELGIUM
4 LUXEMBOURG
5 W. GERMANY
6 E. GERMANY
7 SWITZERLAND
8 AUSTRIA
9 CZECHOSLOVAKIA
10 HUNGARY

11 YUGOSLAVIA
12 ALBANIA
13 CYPRUS
14 LEBANON
15 ISRAEL
16 SYRIA
17 JORDAN
18 KUWAIT
19 BAHRAIN
20 UNITED ARAB EMIRATES

Countries of the World

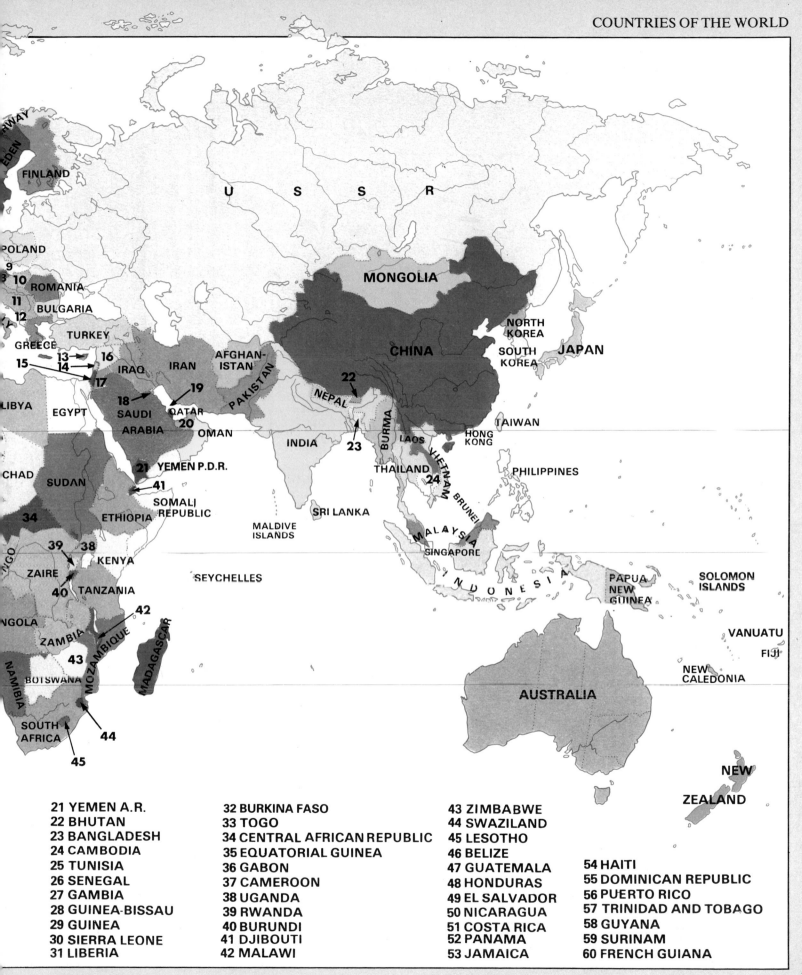

RWAY
EDEN
FINLAND

POLAND
9
8 10
ROMANIA
11
BULGARIA
12
TURKEY
GREECE
13 → 16
15 →
14 →
17
IRAQ
IRAN
AFGHAN-ISTAN
18 → 19
LIBYA
EGYPT
SAUDI
QATAR
ARABIA
20
OMAN
PAKISTAN
INDIA
21 YEMEN P.D.R.
41
CHAD
SUDAN
SOMALI
REPUBLIC
34
ETHIOPIA
39 38
NGO
ZAIRE
KENYA
40 TANZANIA
42
NGOLA
ZAMBIA
43
MADAGASCAR
NAMIBIA
BOTSWANA
SOUTH
AFRICA
44
45

U S S R

MONGOLIA

CHINA

NORTH
KOREA
SOUTH
KOREA
JAPAN

TAIWAN

22
NEPAL
BURMA
LAOS
HONG
KONG
23
THAILAND
VIETNAM
24
BRUNEI
PHILIPPINES

SRI LANKA
MALDIVE
ISLANDS
MALAYSIA
SINGAPORE
INDONESIA

SEYCHELLES

PAPUA
NEW
GUINEA
SOLOMON
ISLANDS

VANUATU
FIJI

NEW
CALEDONIA

AUSTRALIA

NEW

ZEALAND

21 YEMEN A.R.	**32 BURKINA FASO**	**43 ZIMBABWE**
22 BHUTAN	**33 TOGO**	**44 SWAZILAND**
23 BANGLADESH	**34 CENTRAL AFRICAN REPUBLIC**	**45 LESOTHO**
24 CAMBODIA	**35 EQUATORIAL GUINEA**	**46 BELIZE**
25 TUNISIA	**36 GABON**	**47 GUATEMALA**
26 SENEGAL	**37 CAMEROON**	**48 HONDURAS**
27 GAMBIA	**38 UGANDA**	**49 EL SALVADOR**
28 GUINEA-BISSAU	**39 RWANDA**	**50 NICARAGUA**
29 GUINEA	**40 BURUNDI**	**51 COSTA RICA**
30 SIERRA LEONE	**41 DJIBOUTI**	**52 PANAMA**
31 LIBERIA	**42 MALAWI**	**53 JAMAICA**

54 HAITI
55 DOMINICAN REPUBLIC
56 PUERTO RICO
57 TRINIDAD AND TOBAGO
58 GUYANA
59 SURINAM
60 FRENCH GUIANA

The Continents

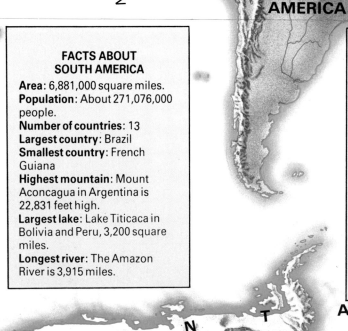

NORTH

AMERICA

ATLANTIC OCEAN

TROPIC OF CANCER

P A C I F I C

O C E A N

EQUATOR

SOUTH

AMERICA   TROPIC OF CAPRICORN

A R

A   N   T   A   R   C

FACTS ABOUT EUROPE
(including all the U.S.S.R.)

Area: Europe (apart from the U.S.S.R.) is 1,882,000 square miles. The U.S.S.R. is 8,650,000 square miles.
Population: Europe, about 485,000,000 people. The U.S.S.R., 262,436,227 people.
Number of countries: 33
Largest country: The U.S.S.R. which is in Europe and Asia.
Smallest country: Vatican City
Highest mountain: Mount Elbrus in the Caucasus Mountains in the U.S.S.R., 18,510 feet.
Largest lake: The Caspian Sea, 143,243 square miles.
Longest rivers: The Ob-Irtysh in the U.S.S.R. is 3,362 miles, the Yenisei is 3,100 miles, and the Volga is 2,194 miles. The Danube, which flows from Germany to the Black Sea, is 1,775 miles.

FACTS ABOUT NORTH &
CENTRAL AMERICA

Area: 9,363,000 square miles including North and Central America, the West Indies, and Greenland.
Population: About 400,000,000 people.
Number of countries: 22
Largest country: Canada
Smallest country: St. Kitts and Nevis
Highest mountain: Mount McKinley in Alaska, 20,320 feet.
Largest lake: Lake Superior, 31,820 square miles.
Longest rivers: Mississippi-Missouri-Red Rock (U.S.A.) 3,741 miles. Mackenzie-Peace-Finlay (Canada) 2,635 miles.

FACTS ABOUT
SOUTH AMERICA

Area: 6,881,000 square miles.
Population: About 271,076,000 people.
Number of countries: 13
Largest country: Brazil
Smallest country: French Guiana
Highest mountain: Mount Aconcagua in Argentina is 22,831 feet high.
Largest lake: Lake Titicaca in Bolivia and Peru, 3,200 square miles.
Longest river: The Amazon River is 3,915 miles.

FACTS ABOUT AFRICA

Area: 11,688,000 square miles.
Population: About 550,500,000 people.
Number of countries: 53
Largest country: Sudan
Smallest country: Seychelles
Highest mountain: Mount Kilimanjaro in Tanzania is 19,340 feet high.
Largest lake: Lake Victoria in Kenya, Tanzania, and Uganda covers 26,724 square miles.
Longest rivers: The river Nile is 4,145 miles long. It is the longest river in the world. The Zaire is 2,718 miles, and the Niger 2,548 miles.

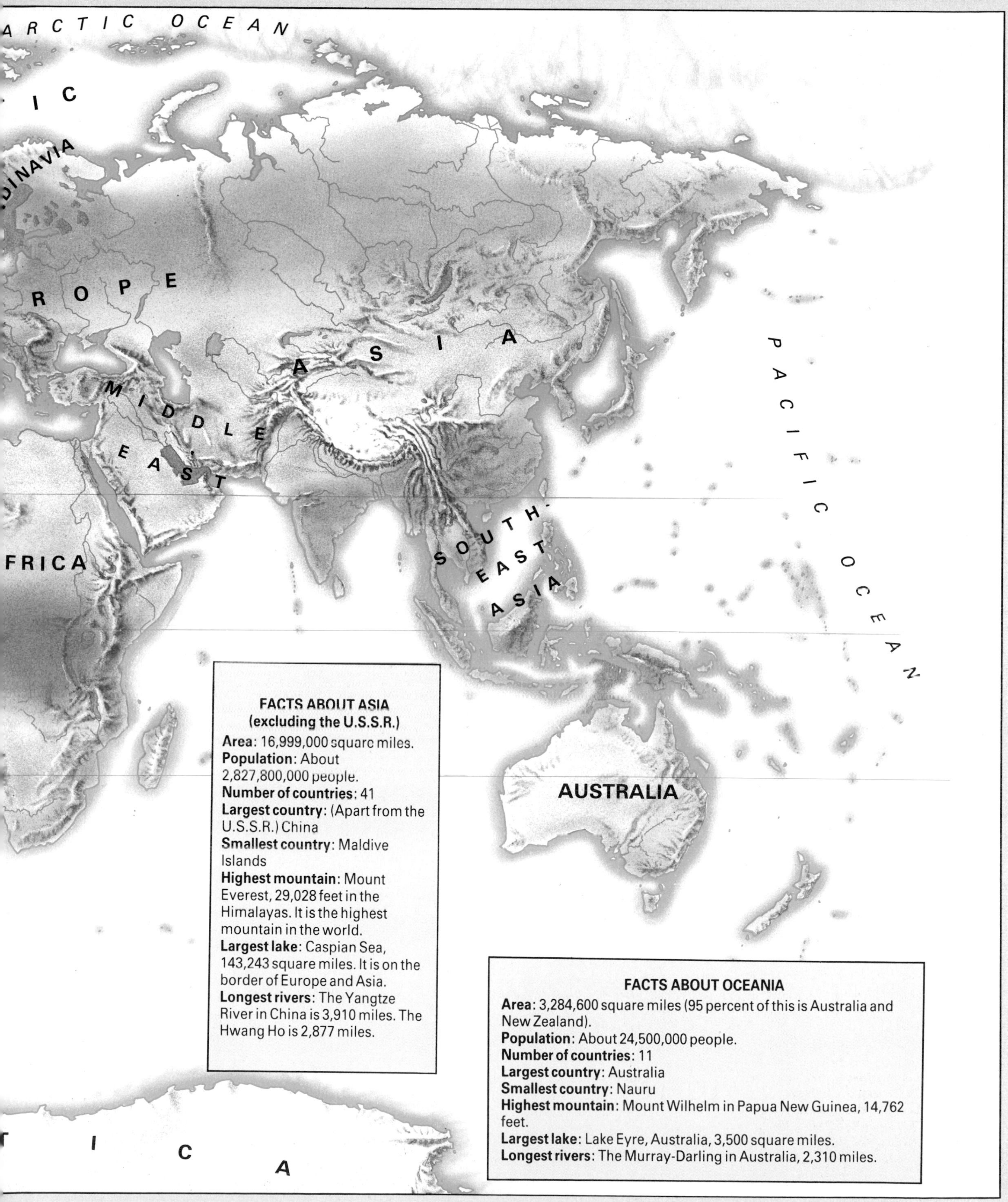

ARCTIC OCEAN

IC

NAVIA

ROPE

MIDDLE

EAST

ASIA

SOUTH-EAST ASIA

PACIFIC OCEAN

FRICA

AUSTRALIA

FACTS ABOUT ASIA
(excluding the U.S.S.R.)
Area: 16,999,000 square miles.
Population: About
2,827,800,000 people.
Number of countries: 41
Largest country: (Apart from the
U.S.S.R.) China
Smallest country: Maldive
Islands
Highest mountain: Mount
Everest, 29,028 feet in the
Himalayas. It is the highest
mountain in the world.
Largest lake: Caspian Sea,
143,243 square miles. It is on the
border of Europe and Asia.
Longest rivers: The Yangtze
River in China is 3,910 miles. The
Hwang Ho is 2,877 miles.

FACTS ABOUT OCEANIA
Area: 3,284,600 square miles (95 percent of this is Australia and
New Zealand).
Population: About 24,500,000 people.
Number of countries: 11
Largest country: Australia
Smallest country: Nauru
Highest mountain: Mount Wilhelm in Papua New Guinea, 14,762
feet.
Largest lake: Lake Eyre, Australia, 3,500 square miles.
Longest rivers: The Murray-Darling in Australia, 2,310 miles.

TIC

A

Scandinavia and Finland

Thousands of years ago Scandinavia was covered with ice sheets and glaciers. These cut deep *fjords* into the coastline and formed many lakes and islands. Iceland is the most northern country in Europe. It still has many snowfields. It is also dotted with many hot springs, steaming geysers and over a hundred volcanoes.

Most Scandinavians enjoy a high standard of living. Sweden is the largest and richest of the countries. Over half the Swedish people live in modern cities, such as Stockholm and Göteborg. Many earn their living by manufacturing paper and other wood products. Sweden, Norway, and Finland have large areas of forest.

Scandinavia's coastal waters teem with fish. Fishermen, mainly from Iceland and Norway, catch large quantities of cod and herring, which are canned or frozen in fish-processing factories.

Dairy farming is important in Denmark. Only one fifth of the people are farmers, but they use the latest machinery and farming methods.

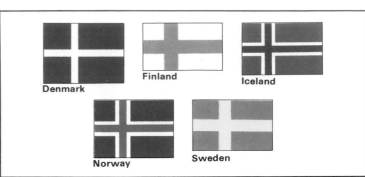

Denmark Finland Iceland

Norway Sweden

Above: The Copenhagen waterfront is very busy. Fishing, shipping, and tourism are important industries in Denmark.

Left: There are hundreds of fjords in Norway. The force of the water falling down cliffs is used to make electricity.

Right: The sculpture in Copenhagen harbor is called the *Little Mermaid* after the fairy tale by Hans Christian Andersen.

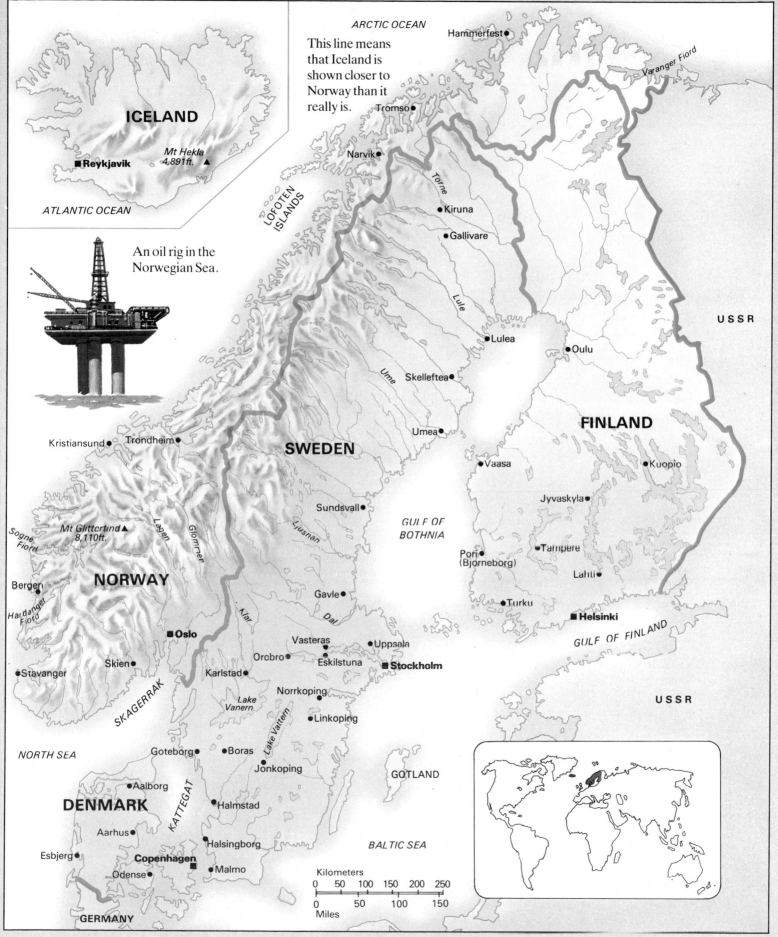

ICELAND

Mt Hekla
4,891ft. ▲

■ Reykjavik

ATLANTIC OCEAN

ARCTIC OCEAN

Hammerfest ●

This line means
that Iceland is
shown closer to
Norway than it
really is.

Varanger Fiord

Tromso ●

Narvik ●

LOFOTEN ISLANDS

Torne

Kiruna ●

Gallivare ●

Lule

USSR

An oil rig in the
Norwegian Sea.

Lulea ●

Oulu ●

Ume

Skelleftea ●

FINLAND

Kristiansund ●   Trondheim ●

Umea ●

SWEDEN

Vaasa ●

Kuopio ●

Mt Glittertind ▲
8,110ft.

Legen

Glommen

Sundsvall ●

GULF OF
BOTHNIA

Jyvaskyla ●

Tampere ●

Sogne
Fiord

NORWAY

Ljusnan

Pori ●
(Bjorneborg)

Lahti ●

Bergen ●

Hardanger
Fiord

Gavle ●

Dal

Turku ●

■ Helsinki

Klar

■ Oslo

GULF OF FINLAND

Skien ●

Vasteras ●   Uppsala ●

● Stavanger

Orebro ●   Eskilstuna ●   ■ Stockholm

USSR

Karlstad ●

Norrkoping ●

SKAGERRAK

Lake
Vanern

Linkoping ●

NORTH SEA

Goteborg ●   ● Boras

Lake Vattern

GOTLAND

Jonkoping ●

● Aalborg

KATTEGAT

Halmstad ●

DENMARK

Aarhus ●

Halsingborg ●

Esbjerg ●

BALTIC SEA

Copenhagen ■   ● Malmo

Odense ●

Kilometers
0 50 100 150 200 250

0 50 100 150
Miles

GERMANY

15

Netherlands, Belgium, and Luxembourg

Netherlands   Belgium   Luxembourg

The Netherlands, Belgium, and Luxembourg are known as the Low Countries because much of the land is flat and below sea level. In the Netherlands high *dikes*, or sea walls, have been built around low-lying lands, which are called *polders*. Nearly a quarter of the Netherlands' land has been *reclaimed*, or taken back, from the sea in this way.

The Low Countries have a combined population of nearly 25 million. This makes them the most densely populated group of countries in Europe. They are also wealthy countries. Most people work in offices and factories, often in textile and electrical companies. Others work on the land. The farms are small and very modern. Dutch farmers grow either flowers or vegetables or keep cows. There are also large iron and steel mills in Belgium and Luxembourg. Luxembourgers are *bilingual*. They speak two languages— French and Luxemburgish.

Below left: A flower market and many beautiful old buildings can be found in the Grand Place of Brussels. Brussels is the headquarters of the Common Market (E.E.C.).

Below: Windmills are often seen in the Dutch countryside. They were once used to pump water from polders to stop flooding.

Cheeses like Edam and Gouda are made in the Netherlands. They are sold in cheese markets.

Today pumping stations pump water from the drainage channels in polders up to the main canal.

NORTH SEA

Ijsselmeer

•Groningen

Haarlem

Amsterdam

NETHERLANDS

Enschede•

Issel

's-Gravenhage
(The Hague)•

Leiden

•Utrecht

Arnhem

Rhine

Rotterdam

Waal

•Dordrecht

Nijmegen•

Maas

•'s-Hertogenbosch

Breda•

•Tilburg

•Eindhoven

WEST GERMANY

Ostend •

Bruges

•Antworp

Ghent

Heerlen-Kerkrasc•

Maastricht•

Lys

Schelde

Brussels

Liege•

BELGIUM

Meuse

•Mons

Charler

•Namur

0 Kilometers — 50

0 Miles — 30

A r d e n n e s

FRANCE

LUXEMBOURG

Luxembourg

The British Isles

The British Isles is made up of two countries: the United Kingdom and the Republic of Ireland. The United Kingdom consists of Great Britain (England, Wales, and Scotland) and Northern Ireland. Many people call the United Kingdom simply Britain. The Republic of Ireland or Eire was once part of the United Kingdom. But in 1921 it became a separate country.

A moist climate makes Britain and the Republic of Ireland ideal for farming. But in Britain one third of the food must still be *imported*, or bought from other countries. The farms are too small to feed the large population.

Industry is very important in Britain. For every one person working on the land, there are ten people living and working in cities. Britain pays for the food it imports by selling manufactured products, such as cars, to other countries.

Britain is divided into many different districts with their own customs and *dialects*, or ways of speaking. In Wales children learn Welsh as well as English in schools.

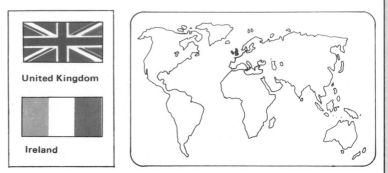

United Kingdom

Ireland

Above: The Houses of Parliament stand beside the river Thames in London. London is the capital of the United Kingdom.

Left: Fishguard is on the coast of south Wales. Most Welsh people live in cities in the south because the north is mountainous.

Below: Eilean Donan Castle is in northwest Scotland.

ORKNEY ISLANDS

SHETLAND ISLANDS

John o' Groats

HEBRIDES

Northwest Highlands

Inverness
Loch Ness
Dee
Aberdeen

▲Ben Nevis 1347m

Grampians

Tay

Oban
Dundee
SCOTLAND Perth

Loch Lomond

Dunfermline

Glasgow
Clyde
Edinburgh

Ayr

A Scottish trawler

An oil-rig explores the British oil field in the North Sea.

Londonderry

NORTHERN IRELAND

Belfast

Tyne

Newcastle
Sunderland

Pennines

Eden

Middlesbrough and Teesside

NORTH SEA

Sligo

Lake District

ISLE OF MAN

Lough Mask

York

Central Plains

Blackpool
Bradford
Leeds
Hull

Galway

Dublin ■

IRISH SEA

Manchester

Liverpool

Sheffield

Shannon
Lough Derg

REPUBLIC OF IRELAND (EIRE)

Limerick

Barrow

Wicklow Mts

▲Snowdon 1086m

Nottingham
Stoke-on-Trent
Wolverhampton

Trent

Cambrian Mts

Dudley
Walsall
Birmingham
Leicester

The Fens

Norwich
Great Yarmouth

Mts of Kerry

Waterford

Coventry
Bedford
Cambridge
Ipswich

Cork

Ouse

Severn

Avon

ENGLAND

Fishguard

WALES

Cotswolds

Oxford

Chiltern Hills

Thames

London ■

ATLANTIC

Swansea

Bristol

North Downs
Canterbury

Cardiff
Bath

Dover

OCEAN

Exmoor

Southampton
Portsmouth
Brighton
Eastbourne

Exeter
Dartmoor

Bournemouth
Isle of Wight

Plymouth

Kilometers
0 20 40 60 80 100

0   25   50
Miles

ISLES OF SCILLY

Land's End

ENGLISH CHANNEL

FRANCE

CHANNEL ISLANDS

France

France is the largest country in Europe, except for the U.S.S.R. Along most of its borders there are mountain ranges. The Jura Mountains separate France from Switzerland, the Pyrenees separate it from Spain, and the Vosges separate France partly from Germany. The Alps border France with Italy and contain Mont Blanc, which is the highest peak in France.

Although many French people work in factories, farming is very important. The warm climate and rich soil help farmers to grow cereals, fruit, and sugar beet. Grapes, used for making wine, are grown in most regions. But the main grapevine growing areas are in Bordeaux, Burgundy, and Champagne. Dairy farming is also important and over 300 different cheeses are made.

Paris, Lyon, and Marseille are the main cities in France. Painters and writers from all over the world have lived in Paris. Many tourists go there today to see its historic buildings, which include the Louvre, the Notre Dame cathedral, and the Eiffel Tower.

France

Monaco

Workers making Renault cars in a huge factory near Paris.

The Eiffel Tower was built in 1889 for the Great Exhibition. It is made of iron and is 1,312 feet high. A spectacular view of Paris can be seen from the higher levels of the tower.

The beautiful Chateau de Chenonceaux is in the Loire Valley. Moats were built around many chateaux to protect them from invaders.

GREAT BRITAIN

NORTH SEA

Kilometers
0   50   100   150   200
0   50   100   150
Miles

ENGLISH CHANNEL

Dunkerque
Calais
Boulogne
Roubaix
Lille
Valenciennes
Douai
BELGIUM

LUXEM-
BOURG

GERMANY

Dieppe
Somme
Amiens
Cherbourg
Le Havre
Oise
Meuse
Channel Islands
Rouen
Caen
Seine
Reims
Metz
Nancy
Strasbourg
Brest
Marne
Paris
Versailles
Champagne
Vosges Mts
Chartres
Fontainebleau
Rennes
Le Mans
Mulhouse
Orleans
Loire
Saone
FRANCE
Angers
Tours
Dijon
Nantes
SWITZERLAND
Limoges
Jura Mts
Lyon
Mt Blanc
15,771ft.
Clermont-Ferrand
Mt Dore
6,188ft.
Saint-Etienne
Grenoble
Périgueux
Massif Central
ITALY
Bordeaux
Dordogne
French Alps
Cevennes Mts
Garonne
Rhône
Nimes
Avignon
Toulouse
Montpellier
Arles
Nice
MONACO
Bayonne
Biarritz
Marseille
Cannes
Lourdes
Carcassonne
Toulon
Pyrenees
Narbonne
Perpignan
ANDORRA
MEDITERRANEAN SEA
SPAIN

BAY OF BISCAY

8,891ft.
CORSICA
(France)

Corsica is an island
belonging to France. To
see its proper location
turn to page 29.

21

Germany: West and East

Since 1945 Germany has been divided into West Germany and East Germany. West Germany's proper name is the Federal Republic of Germany. East Germany's proper name is the German Democratic Republic. The city of Berlin is also divided into east and west *zones*. In 1961 a wall was built along East Berlin's boundaries to stop people crossing into West Germany.

The Germans are well-organized and hard-working people. Since 1945 large numbers of factories have been set up in both East and West Germany. These manufacture everything from steel to textiles. In West Germany workers in the industrial Ruhr Valley make cars, heavy machinery, cables, and electrical equipment. Today West Germany is one of the wealthiest countries in Europe.

Farming as well as manufacturing is important in East Germany. There are also many *lignite* mines. Lignite is a type of coal. East Germany is the world's chief supplier of lignite. Workers mine around 250 million tons of it every year.

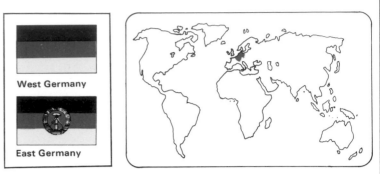

West Germany

East Germany

Above: Hamburg is a major docking point in the North Sea.

Left: Before the Berlin Wall was built, the Brandenburg Gate was the main thoroughfare between East and West Berlin.

Below: Barges travel down the Rhine in West Germany past lovely towns and castles, green fields, and vineyards.

Kilometers
0   50   100   150
0   30   60   90
Miles

NORTH SEA

Kiel

Kiel Canal

Rostock

Lubeck

Hamburg

Elbe

POLAND

Bremen

Oder

Ems

Aller

Oder

Weser

Berlin

Hanover

Brunswick

Magdeburg

EAST GERMANY

NETHERLANDS

Spree

Munster

Bielefeld

Harz Mts

Rhine

Dortmund

Halle

Elbe

Essen   Bochum

Leipzig

Duisburg

Ruhr

Krefeld   Wuppertal

Kassel

Monchen-gladbach   Dusseldorf

Dresden

Cologne

Karl-Marx-Stadt

Aachen

Bonn

BELGIUM

WEST GERMANY

Mosel

Wiesbaden   Frankfurt

Mainz

LUXEMBOURG

Main

CZECHOSLOVAKIA

Mannheim

Nuremberg

Saarbrucken

Rhine

Karlsruhe

Danube

Stuttgart

Black Forest

FRANCE

Augsburg

Munich

SWITZERLAND

AUSTRIA

23

Switzerland and Austria

Switzerland and Austria are well known for their snowcapped mountains called the Alps. The Alps attract many visitors who like to ski in the winter and visit lakes, glaciers, and alpine meadows full of wild flowers in the summer. Long tunnels and bridges take roads and railroads through the mountains and valleys.

In Switzerland rivers are dammed to catch water and make electricity for homes and factories. This is called *hydroelectricity*. Many Swiss people work in factories making chemicals, scientific instruments, clocks and watches, and delicious chocolate. Banks and hotels provide important jobs.

Most Swiss people speak German, but French, Italian, and Romansch are also spoken.

Austria was part of a large and important country called the Austro-Hungarian Empire until 1918. Now it is quite small. Austria has some minerals such as iron and oil, but tourism is also very important. Most Austrians live in towns. Vienna, the capital, is famous for its music. In the past famous musicians such as Beethoven and Mozart have lived and composed music there.

Sandwiched between Austria and Switzerland is the tiny country of Liechtenstein.

Holiday resorts in Switzerland are well known for their fresh mountain air and clear lakes. In the summer, boating and mountain climbing are popular activities.

Switzerland   Austria

Left: Among the many large lakes in Switzerland is Lake Luzern.

Right: Ice skating out of doors is possible for many months in alpine countries.

Below: An outdoor cafe in a busy Vienna shopping district provides a meeting place for friends.

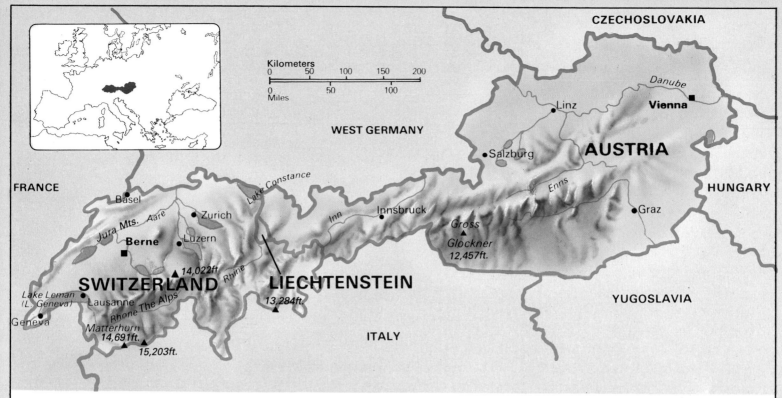

CZECHOSLOVAKIA

WEST GERMANY

Danube

Linz

Vienna

Salzburg

AUSTRIA

FRANCE

Basel

Zurich

Jura Mts. Aare

Berne

Luzern

Lake Constance

Inn

Innsbruck

Enns

Gross
Glockner
12,457ft.

HUNGARY

Graz

SWITZERLAND

14,022ft

Rhine

LIECHTENSTEIN
13,284ft.

YUGOSLAVIA

Lake Leman
(L. Geneva)

Lausanne

Rhone The Alps

Geneva

Matterhorn
14,691ft.

15,203ft.

ITALY

Kilometers
0   50   100   150   200

Miles
0   50   100

Spain and Portugal

Spain's interior is a vast *plateau*, which means an area of high flat ground. It is crossed by several mountain ranges. But the highest peaks are in the Pyrenees in the north and the Sierra Nevada in the south. Fertile plains and sandy beaches surround the central plateau. Spain is divided into several regions. One of these is Andalusia in the south. It is famous for its lively fiestas and gypsy flamenco dancers.

Spain's warm climate and golden sands attract thousands of tourists to its coastal resorts. Many Spaniards work in the tourist industry, but most work on the land. Some farmers do everything by hand or with the help of a donkey or mule. The soil is very dry and needs to be constantly watered, or *irrigated*. Farmers grow wheat, rice, olives, grapes, and oranges.

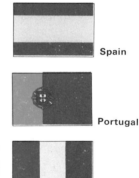

Spain

Portugal

Andorra

Portugal borders Spain on the west. Most people are fishermen and farmers. Others work in the tourist industry or in factories where they process food and make textiles. There are large cork forests in Portugal and many vineyards. Cork and port, a special type of wine, are exported to countries all over the world.

Top: Roman walls surround a city in Castile, a region in central Spain. The Romans ruled in Spain for six hundred years.

Middle: Workers in Portugal gather bark from cork trees to make cork.

Far left: Tourists relax on the warm, sunny beaches of Ibiza.

Left: A fisherman mends his net in Albufeira, Portugal. Huge numbers of sardines are caught off Portugal's coast.

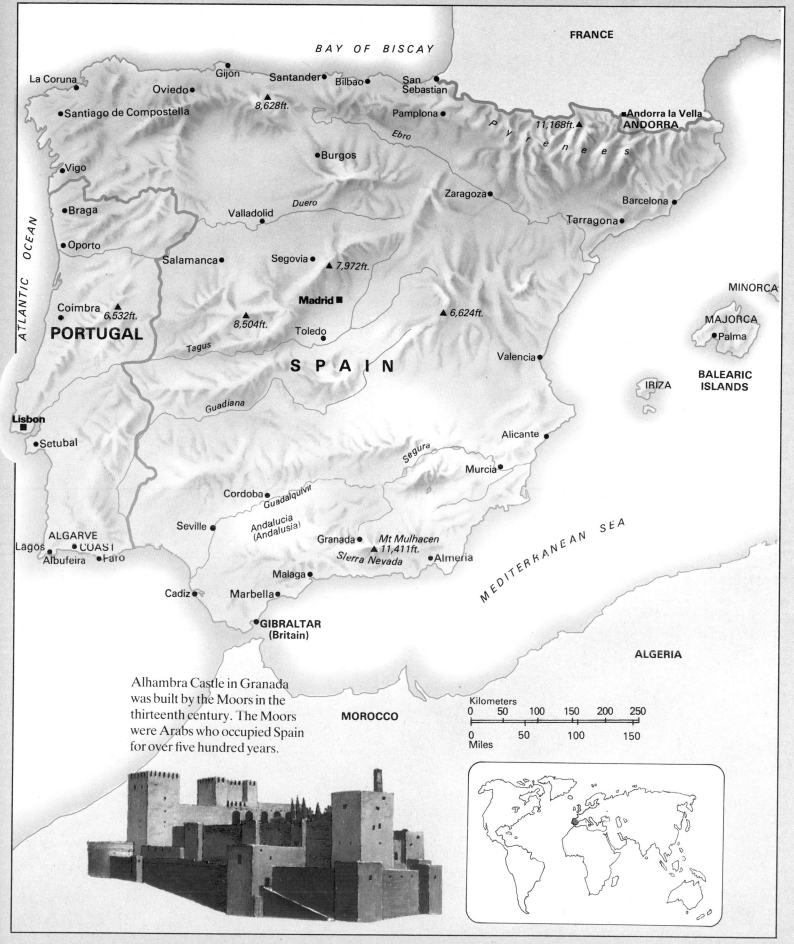

FRANCE

BAY OF BISCAY

La Coruna

Gijon

Santander

Bilbao

San Sebastian

Andorra la Vella
ANDORRA

Oviedo

▲ *8,628ft.*

Pamplona

Pyrenees

11,168ft. ▲

Santiago de Compostella

Ebro

Burgos

Vigo

Zaragoza

Barcelona

Braga

Duero

Valladolid

Tarragona

Oporto

Salamanca

Segovia

▲ *7,972ft.*

MINORCA

ATLANTIC OCEAN

Coimbra

▲ *6,532ft.*

Madrid ■

▲ *6,624ft.*

MAJORCA

Palma

PORTUGAL

▲ *8,504ft.*

Toledo

Tagus

S P A I N

Valencia

**BALEARIC
ISLANDS**

Guadiana

IBIZA

Lisbon ■

Setubal

Alicante

Segura

Murcia

Cordoba

Guadalquivir

MEDITERRANEAN SEA

ALGARVE

Seville

Andalucia
(Andalusia)

Granada

Mt Mulhacen
▲ *11,411ft.*

Sierra Nevada

Almeria

Lagos

COAST

Faro

Albufeira

Malaga

Cadiz

Marbella

●**GIBRALTAR**
(Britain)

ALGERIA

Alhambra Castle in Granada
was built by the Moors in the
thirteenth century. The Moors
were Arabs who occupied Spain
for over five hundred years.

MOROCCO

Kilometers

0   50   100   150   200   250

0   50   100   150
Miles

Italy and Its Neighbors

Italy is shaped like a boot kicking a ball. Sicily is the "ball." Sicily, Sardinia, and many smaller islands are also part of Italy. The Apennine Mountains run down the back of Italy like a spine. There are several volcanic mountains in Italy. The best known is Mount Vesuvius, near the city of Naples in southern Italy.

Tourists flock to Italy to enjoy the warm climate, to see the beautiful buildings and paintings, and to visit the ruins of ancient Rome. In the north there are large industrial cities, such as Milan and Turin. Italians make textiles and cars for *export*, to sell to other countries. In the south farmers grow olives, citrus fruit, and grapes for making wine.

Vatican City is the smallest country in Europe. It is the home of the Pope, the head of the Roman Catholic Church. San Marino is another tiny country in Italy and Malta is an island country in the Mediterranean Sea.

Italy

San Marino

Vatican City

Malta

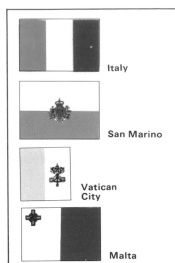

Above: St. Peter's Square is in Vatican City.
Left: Venice has many fine churches like Santa Maria della Salute. Boats called *gondolas* take people from place to place on canals that run through the city.
Right: The Leaning Tower of Pisa.

AUSTRIA

SWITZERLAND

13,432ft.

Lake Como

▲ *15,203ft.*

▲ *13,323ft.*

Milan ●   Brescia ●

Lake Garda

Verona ●   Padua ●   ● Venice

● Trieste

Turin ●

Po

▲ *12,602ft.*

Parma ●   ● Ferrara

Modena ●

▲ *10,817ft.*   Genoa ●   ● Bologna

FRANCE

ITALY

7,103ft.▲   ● Rimini

Florence ●   **SAN MARINO**

Pisa ●

Livorno ●   Siena ●

LIGURIAN SEA

A   ● Assisi

p   ▲ *8,130ft.*

p   *e*

Tiber   *n*   ▲ *9,560ft.*

▲ *8,891ft.*   *n*

i

CORSICA   *n*

(France)   *i*

Ajaccio ●   **VATICAN CITY STATE**

■ **Rome**   *e*

s

● Sassari

SARDINIA   Bari ●

(Italy)

▲   *4,190ft.*

6,017ft.   Naples ●   ▲ *Mt Vesuvius*   ● Brindisi

● Salerno   Taranto ●

Capri ●

Cagliari ●

TYRRHENIAN SEA

Stromboli

Vulcano

Messina ●   ● Reggio

● Palermo

11,053ft.

▲ *Mt Etna*

SICILY   ● Catania   *MEDITERRANEAN SEA*

ADRIATIC SEA

YUGOSLAVIA

Kilometers

0   50   100   150   200   250

0   50   100   150

Miles

MALTA   ■ **Valetta**

Poland, Czechoslovakia, and Hungary

Poland and Hungary are countries with vast areas of flat land. The fertile lowlands are good for farming and herds of cattle and horses graze on the wide open plains. Between these two countries lies Czechoslovakia. Here the snowcapped Carpathian Mountains tower over the land.

Poland is the largest country. It is a major world producer of coal. There are many big ports on the Baltic Sea where ships are built. Czechoslovakia and Hungary do not have any seaside but the river Danube links them with the sea. Barges carry goods along it to other countries in Europe.

Czechoslovakia, Poland, and Hungary have been *Communist* countries since 1945. In Communist countries, the government runs most factories and mines and many farms. Potatoes, wheat, and sugar beets are important crops on the farms. But since 1945 more and more Poles, Czechs, and Hungarians have been leaving their farms to work in mines and factories.

Poland

Czechoslovakia

Hungary

A view of Prague, capital of Czechoslovakia, in winter.

Above: Czechoslovakia is a country of mountains, basins, and valleys.
Right: Buda and Pest are shown with the river Danube in between. Together they make Budapest, the capital of Hungary.

Kilometers

0   50   100   150   200

Miles

0   50   100

BALTIC SEA

U S S R

Gdansk

Szczecin

Bydgoszcz

Netze

Odr

Poznan

Vistula

Bug

Warta

Warsaw

POLAND

Lodz

Neisse

Wroclaw

Lublin

Workers harvest their crops on a collective farm in Poland.

Katowice

Krakow

Prague

Elbe

4,895ft.

Plzen

Ostrava

WEST
GERMANY

CZECHOSLOVAKIA

Vltava

Carpathian Mts.

Brno

Van

8,711ft.

Kosice

Bratislava

Miskolc

AUSTRIA

Danube

Budapest

Debrecen

Lake
Balaton

Tisza

HUNGARY

ROMANIA

ITALY

Pecs

Szeged

YUGOSLAVIA

31

The Balkans and Romania

Bulgaria, Yugoslavia, Albania, and Greece make up the Balkan countries. Romania borders Bulgaria and Yugoslavia.

Greece consists of the mainland and over 1,400 islands. It is very mountainous and sheep and goats graze over the hills. Only one third of Greece is suitable for farming. But in spite of this, nearly half of the people live on the land. Many farmers grow grapes for making wine. Sometimes the grapes are picked, left to dry in the hot sun, then sold as raisins, currants, or sultanas.

Bulgaria, Yugoslavia, Albania, and Romania are also very mountainous. But, unlike Greece, the mountains are covered with forests where wolves, wild boars, and bears still live. Beneath the valuable forests there are rich deposits of copper, zinc, coal, and oil. Many people work in industry turning these minerals into useful products. Many others, especially in Albania, work on farms in the valleys.

Yugoslavia and Greece have beautiful beaches and islands. Thousands of people vacation there each year. Greece also has fascinating ruins from the times of the ancient Greeks.

Albania   Romania   Bulgaria

Greece   Yugoslavia

Above: The Parthenon in Athens was built by the ancient Greeks.
Left: Many Romanians work on farms growing corn, wheat, and tobacco. They also raise sheep.
Below: Dubrovnik in Yugoslavia is well known for its beaches and medieval buildings.

Kilometers
0 50 100 150 200 250
0 50 100 150
Miles

USSR

HUNGARY

Drava

▲ Mt. Triglav
9,393ft.
Ljubljana

•Zagreb

•Rijeka

Tisa

Sava

•Timisoara

Cluj•

Carpathian Mts.

8,343ft.
▲

•Brasov

Transylvania Alps

Galati•

8,261ft.
▲

■ Belgrade

Turnu
Severin•

ROMANIA

•Ploesti

■ **Bucharest**

YUGOSLAVIA

Dinaric Alps

Sarajevo•

•Split

Morava

•Craiova

Constanta•

Danube

•Ruse

Iskar

*BLACK
SEA*

▲ 8,274ft.

•Dubrovnik

*ADRIATIC
SEA*

•Nis

BULGARIA

Varna•

■ **Sofia**

Balkan Mts.

Burgas•

▲
8,832ft.

8,189ft.
▲

•Skopje

Vardar

Mt.
Musala
9,596ft. ▲

•Marits a

Plovdiv

Rhodope Mts.

■ **Tirana**

8,136ft.
▲

ALBANIA

•Thessaloniki

8,652ft.
▲

Mt.Olympus
▲ 9,570ft.

Pindus Mts.

•Trikkala

GREECE

•Delphi

*AEGEAN
SEA*

LESVOS

TURKEY

•Patras

7,795ft.▲

•Piraeus

Athens ■

Corinth•

IONIAN SEA

•Olympia

MYKONOS

Kalamata•

•Sparta

NAXOS

This picture shows a
windmill on the Greek
island of Mykonos.
Whitewashed buildings
like those in the
background are often
found in Greece.

MEDITERRANEAN SEA

RHODES

CRETE •Iraklion

33

U.S.S.R.

The Union of Soviet Socialist Republics, the U.S.S.R., is the largest country in the world. It is more than twice the size of Canada, the second-largest country, and covers one sixth of the world's total land surface.

Since the Communist revolution in 1917, the U.S.S.R. has developed from an old-fashioned farming country into a powerful industrial nation. It has large *resources* of coal, oil, and natural gas. These provide fuel for the huge numbers of factories and industrial plants. The U.S.S.R., like the United States, has a large space industry. The first man and woman to be launched into space were Russians.

One fourth of the U.S.S.R. is farmland. Farmers work either on enormous state-owned farms or on smaller *collectives*. The U.S.S.R. is a leading producer of wheat, meat, and dairy products. It is divided into fifteen republics. These are made up of people of over a hundred groups—Ukranians, Uzbeks, Kazakhs, and many others. Over sixty languages are used in the U.S.S.R.. But Russian is spoken in most places because the Russian Federal Republic is the largest republic.

Left: Melons are sold at the market in Samarkand in the south of the U.S.S.R.

Right: On huge state farms in the Steppes wheat is harvested by combines. Most people live on farms and in cities west of the Ural Mountains. Farther east, over the mountains, there are high plains and vast forests. The Trans-Siberian Railway runs from Moscow in the west to Vladivostok in the east – over 5,600 miles.

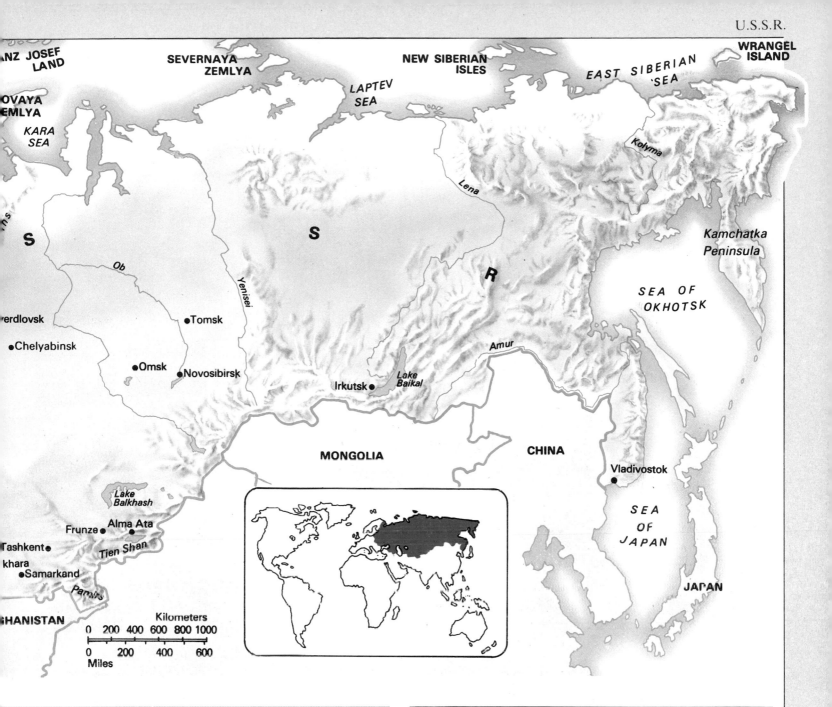

FRANZ JOSEF LAND

SEVERNAYA ZEMLYA

NEW SIBERIAN ISLES

WRANGEL ISLAND

NOVAYA ZEMLYA

KARA SEA

LAPTEV SEA

EAST SIBERIAN SEA

Kolyma

Lena

S

S

R

Kamchatka Peninsula

Ob

Yenisei

Sverdlovsk

Chelyabinsk

Tomsk

Omsk

Novosibirsk

Irkutsk

Lake Baikal

Amur

SEA OF OKHOTSK

MONGOLIA

CHINA

Vladivostok

SEA OF JAPAN

JAPAN

Lake Balkhash

Frunze

Alma Ata

Tashkent

Bukhara

Samarkand

Tien Shan

Pamirs

AFGHANISTAN

Kilometers
0 200 400 600 800 1000

0 200 400 600
Miles

Above: Inside the Kremlin (Russian for *fortress*) is the national museum. Lenin's tomb is in the foreground.
Left: Red Square and St. Basil's Cathedral in Moscow.

35

Southwest Asia

Most people living in the Middle East are Arabs. Their language is Arabic and their religion is Islam. Even in the non-Arab countries, Iran and Turkey, the people are Muslim. Many Christians live in Cyprus and Lebanon and most of the people in Israel are Jewish. The different religions of the people living in this area is the cause of constant trouble between them.

On the map you can see that most of this area is desert. Many of the people are farmers and the lack of rainfall is a serious problem.

On the Mediterranean coast, in river valleys and around *oases*, farms are irrigated with water from rivers and wells. But it is oil and not farming which has brought wealth to many countries in this area.

Every year pilgrims arrive in the Middle East. Jerusalem, the capital of Israel, is regarded as a holy city by Jews, Christians, and Muslims. Mecca and Medina in Saudi Arabia are Muslim holy cities.

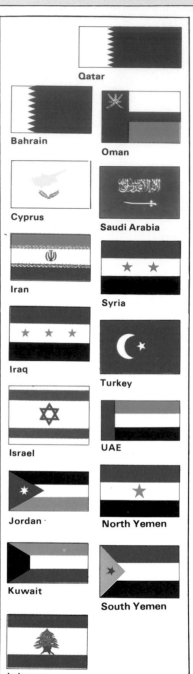

Qatar

Bahrain

Oman

Cyprus

Saudi Arabia

Iran

Syria

Iraq

Turkey

Israel

UAE

Jordan

North Yemen

Kuwait

South Yemen

Lebanon

Above: A road through the desert joins Abu Dhabi and Al Ain in the United Arab Emirates.

Below: Muslims make their pilgrimage to Mecca, birthplace of the prophet Muhammad.

Jews pray at the Western Wall (Wailing Wall) in the Old City of Jerusalem. The Dome of the Rock, sacred to Muslims, is in the background.

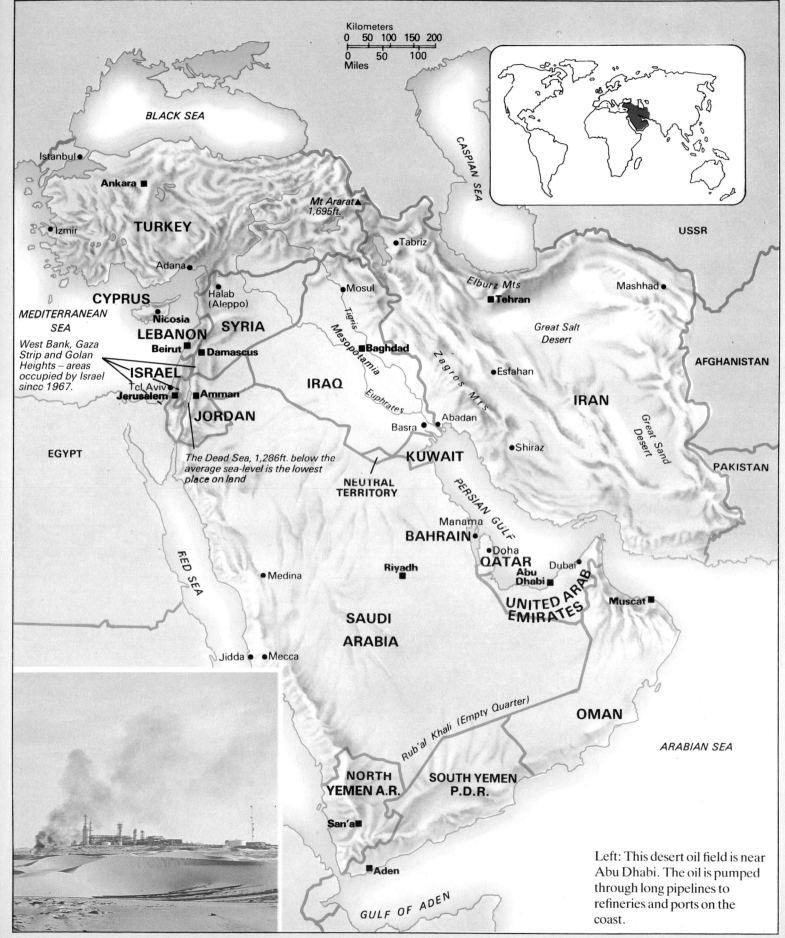

Kilometers
0 50 100 150 200

0   50   100
Miles

BLACK SEA

Istanbul ●

Ankara ■

TURKEY

Izmir ●

Adana ●

Mt Ararat ▲
1,695ft.

Tabriz ●

CASPIAN SEA

USSR

CYPRUS

MEDITERRANEAN
SEA

Halab
(Aleppo) ●

Mosul ●

Elburz Mts

Mashhad ●

Tehran ■

Nicosia ●

SYRIA

LEBANON

Beirut ● ■ Damascus

*West Bank, Gaza
Strip and Golan
Heights – areas
occupied by Israel
since 1967.*

ISRAEL

Tel Aviv ●

Jerusalem ■

Amman ■

JORDAN

EGYPT

*The Dead Sea, 1,286ft. below the
average sea-level is the lowest
place on land*

Tigris

Mesopotamia

Baghdad ■

Euphrates

IRAQ

Zagros Mts

Great Salt
Desert

Esfahan ●

Basra ●

Abadan ●

KUWAIT

NEUTRAL
TERRITORY

Shiraz ●

IRAN

Great Sand
Desert

AFGHANISTAN

PAKISTAN

RED SEA

Medina ●

Riyadh ■

PERSIAN GULF

Manama
BAHRAIN ●

Doha ●

QATAR

Abu
Dhabi ■

Dubai ●

UNITED ARAB
EMIRATES

Muscat ■

SAUDI
ARABIA

Jidda ● ● Mecca

Rub'al Khali (Empty Quarter)

OMAN

ARABIAN SEA

NORTH
YEMEN A.R.

SOUTH YEMEN
P.D.R.

San'a ■

Aden ■

GULF OF ADEN

Left: This desert oil field is near
Abu Dhabi. The oil is pumped
through long pipelines to
refineries and ports on the
coast.

India and Its Neighbors

This region contains the highest mountain range in the world—the Himalayas. It forms the boundary with Tibet and China and contains Mount Everest, the world's highest peak. On the map opposite you can trace the paths of three great rivers. They begin in the Himalayas and are the Ganges, the Indus, and the Brahmaputra.

India, Pakistan, and Bangladesh are thickly populated nations. Farming is the main occupation, but there is never enough food for the huge numbers of people. Many children start to work in the fields with their parents when they are very young. Farming methods are often very simple because there is little money for machinery or fertilizers. The *monsoon* climate is also a problem. It means that twice a year there are huge downpours of rain. If the rain is too heavy, it washes away crops. If the rains come too late, the crops may die. The Indian, Pakistani, and Bangladeshi governments are trying to set up more factories.

Religion is important in the everyday life of the people in this region. Most Indians are Hindu while most Pakistanis and Afghanis and many Bangladeshis are Muslim, followers of Islam.

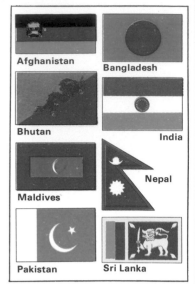

Afghanistan
Bangladesh
Bhutan
India
Maldives
Nepal
Pakistan
Sri Lanka

Above: Pilgrims bathe in the river Ganges at Varanasi, the Hindus' holy city.

Above right: The Taj Mahal is made of white marble. It is the tomb of a Mogul emperor and his favorite wife.

Right: This film poster is in New Delhi. More films are made in India than in any other country.

Far right: Women pick tea leaves in Darjeeling. Behind them is Mount Kanchenjunga.

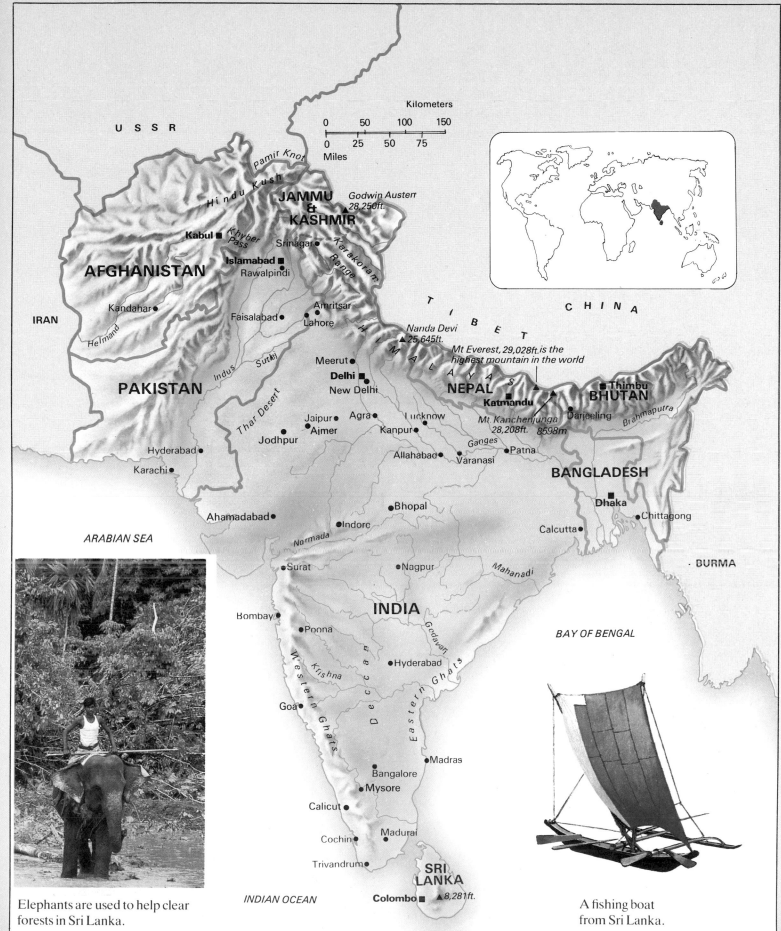

Kilometers
0   50   100   150
0   25   50   75
Miles

U S S R

Pamir Knot

Hindu Kush

JAMMU
& KASHMIR

*Godwin Austen
28,250ft.*

Kabul ■

Khyber Pass

Srinagar ●

Islamabad ■
Rawalpindi ●

AFGHANISTAN

Karakoram Range

IRAN

Kandahar ●

T I B E T

C H I N A

Helmand

Amritsar ●

Faisalabad ●
Lahore ●

*Nanda Devi
25,645ft.*

PAKISTAN

Indus

Sutlej

Meerut ●

H I M A L A Y A S

Mt Everest, 29,028ft. is the
highest mountain in the world

Delhi ■
New Delhi

NEPAL

Thimbu ■
BHUTAN

Thar Desert

Jaipur ●
Ajmer ●

Agra ●

Lucknow ●

Katmandu ■

*Mt. Kanchenjunga
28,208ft.   8598m*

Darjeeling ●

Brahmaputra

Jodhpur ●

Kanpur ●

Hyderabad ●

Allahabad ●

Ganges

Varanasi ●

Patna ●

BANGLADESH

Karachi ●

Ahamadabad ●

Bhopal ●

Dhaka ■

Chittagong ●

ARABIAN SEA

Indore ●

Calcutta ●

Normada

BURMA

Surat ●

Nagpur ●

Mahanadi

INDIA

Bombay ●

BAY OF BENGAL

Poona ●

Godavari

Western Ghats

Krishna

Hyderabad ●

Deccan

Eastern Ghats

Goa ●

Madras ●

Bangalore ●
Mysore ●

Calicut ●

Cochin ●

Madurai ●

Trivandrum ●

SRI
LANKA

INDIAN OCEAN

Colombo ■   ▲8,281ft.

Elephants are used to help clear
forests in Sri Lanka.

A fishing boat
from Sri Lanka.

39

China

Nearly a fourth of all the people in the world live in China. It has more people than any other nation. Most people live in the fertile valleys of the Hwang Ho and Yangtze rivers and along the crowded coast. China is the third-largest country in the world. It stretches from the plateau of central Asia to the Pacific Ocean.

Since 1949 China has had a Communist government. Mao Zedong (Mao Tse-tung) was the leader of the government until his death in 1976. By encouraging everyone to put the needs of the community first, he helped turn China from a poor agricultural country into a great industrial one. Factories have been built all over China and many of the workers make iron and steel. But farming is still important and two thirds of the people are farmers.

Mongolia lies to the north of China. Most of the country is desert and the few people living there are wandering herdsmen. Many of them live in tents. On the map you can also see the peninsula of Korea. It is divided into two countries—North Korea and South Korea.

China

Mongolia

North Korea

South Korea

Above: The Great Wall of China is 1,490 miles long. It was built 2,500 years ago to keep Mongol invaders out.

Above right: A junk in Causeway Bay. Hong Kong has been a British colony for many years, but in 1997 it will return to China.

Right: Herdsmen in Mongolia lay the foundations for a tent, or *yurt*.

40

Kilometers
0 200 400 600

0 100 200 300
Miles

USSR

MANCHURIA

Ulan Bator

MONGOLIA

Chichihaerh
(Tsitsihar)

Haerbpin
(Harbin)

Altai Mts.

Urunqi

Shan

Gobi Desert

Hsi-Liao

Chilin
(Kirin)

Shenyang • Fushun

Anshan

NORTH
KOREA

INNER MONGOLIA

Huhhot

Kalgan

Tarim Basin

Paotou

Beijing
(Peking)

Tangshan

Tianjin

Luta

Pyongyang

Great Wall of China

Nan Shan

Yinchuan

Shijiazhuang

Taiyuan

Jinan
(Tsinan)

(Tientsin)

Poshan

Tsingtao

Seoul

SOUTH
KOREA

Pusan

Altyn Tagh

Shan

Lonzhou

YELLOW SEA

Hwang Ho

Hsian
(Sian)

Paoki

Loyang

Zhengzhou

Suchow

TIBET

Salween

CHINA

Mekong

Chengdu

Yangtze Kiang

Hefei

Nanjing

Soochow

Shanghai

Hangzhou

ngpao (Brahmaputra)

st
ft.

Lhasa

Chungking

Wuhan

EAST CHINA SEA

BHUTAN

Ipin

Changsha

Nanchang

Guiyang

Fuzhou

Taipei

BANGLADESH

Kunming

Si-Kiang

TAIWAN

Kaohsiung

Nanning

Guangzhou
(Canton)

MACAO
(Portugal)

HONG KONG
(Britain)

PACIFIC OCEAN

BURMA

VIETNAM

LAOS

SOUTH CHINA SEA

HAINAN

41

Japan

Japan consists of four main islands and about 3,000 smaller ones. From one end of the main islands to the other, there runs a volcanic mountain chain. Many of the volcanoes are still active. Mount Fuji, the highest peak, is a volcano, but it has not erupted since 1707. Earthquakes are common in Japan. There are over 1,000 each year, but most of them are only small tremors.

There is not much land suitable for farming in Japan because it is so mountainous. Rice is the main food crop on the little land which is cultivated. Fishing is important, for it provides food for the large population. Japanese cooks use shark fins and eels to make soup and seaweed is also a favorite dish.

Japan is the wealthiest country in Asia because it has an efficient manufacturing industry. Japanese workers make more cameras, television sets, and ships than any other country. There are many crowded industrial cities in Japan. But there are also peaceful temples and beautiful gardens.

Top: Television sets are checked on a conveyor belt in a Japanese factory. Other factories make cars, computers, watches, calculators, and stereos.

Above: Workers harvest rice in Japan. Rice grows well on flat land where there is heavy rainfall.

Left: The bullet train is also called the "Hikari Express." It is the world's fastest passenger train and it travels between Tokyo and Osaka. Mount Fuji is in the background.

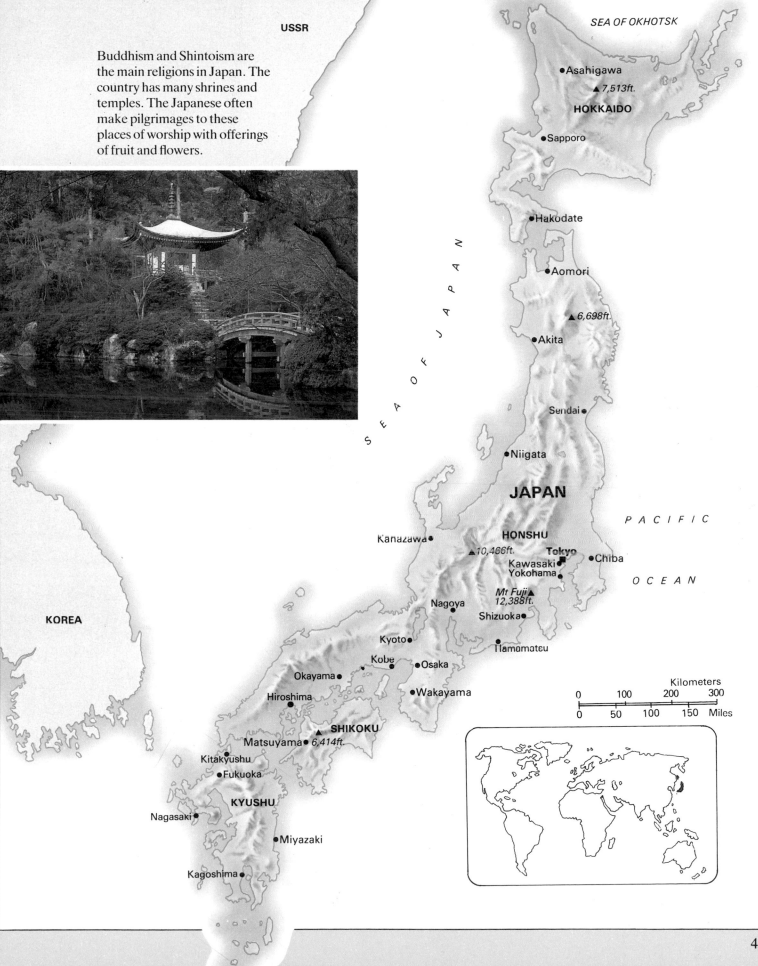

Buddhism and Shintoism are the main religions in Japan. The country has many shrines and temples. The Japanese often make pilgrimages to these places of worship with offerings of fruit and flowers.

USSR

SEA OF OKHOTSK

•Asahigawa
▲ 7,513ft.
HOKKAIDO

•Sapporo

•Hakodate

•Aomori

▲ 6,698ft.

•Akita

SEA OF JAPAN

•Sendai

•Niigata

JAPAN

HONSHU

Kanazawa•

▲10,466ft.

Tokyo
Kawasaki •Chiba
Yokohama

PACIFIC

OCEAN

Nagoya•

Mt Fuji▲
12,388ft.

Shizuoka•

Kyoto•

Hamamatsu•

KOREA

Kobe• •Osaka

Okayama•

Hiroshima•

•Wakayama

SHIKOKU

Matsuyama• ▲6,414ft.

Kitakyushu•

•Fukuoka

KYUSHU

Nagasaki•

•Miyazaki

Kagoshima•

Kilometers
0   100   200   300
0   50   100   150 Miles

Southeast Asia

Much of Southeast Asia is made up of volcanic islands. Indonesia has over 3,000 islands and the Philippines more than 7,000. All the countries have a similar hot, wet climate and much of the land is mountainous.

Southeast Asia is a heavily populated region. Many people live in stilt houses in fertile river valleys. Peasant farmers cut terraces into the hillsides where they grow rice, the main food crop. The slopes which are not tilled are covered in forest. There are also large rubber, coffee, and tobacco plantations in Indonesia, Malaysia, and Burma.

Mining is another important occupation in this region. Malaysia produces one third of the world's supply of tin. It is one of the richest countries in Southeast Asia. But many people in Vietnam and its neighboring countries are very poor because of years of war.

Music, dance, drama, and handmade crafts keep alive the ancient stories and legends of Southeast Asia. Islam and Buddhism are the main religions in this area.

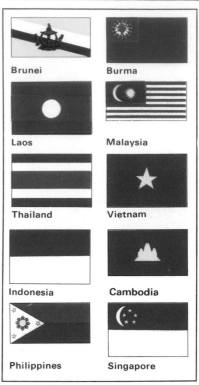

Brunei • Burma • Laos • Malaysia • Thailand • Vietnam • Indonesia • Cambodia • Philippines • Singapore

Left: Fruit and vegetables are paddled in from the countryside and sold at the floating market in Bangkok. The many canals in the city are called *klongs*.

Right: Rice grows in paddies on terraced hillsides in the Philippines. It has been grown this way for hundreds of years.

Below: Huge figures of demons guard a Buddhist temple in Bangkok.

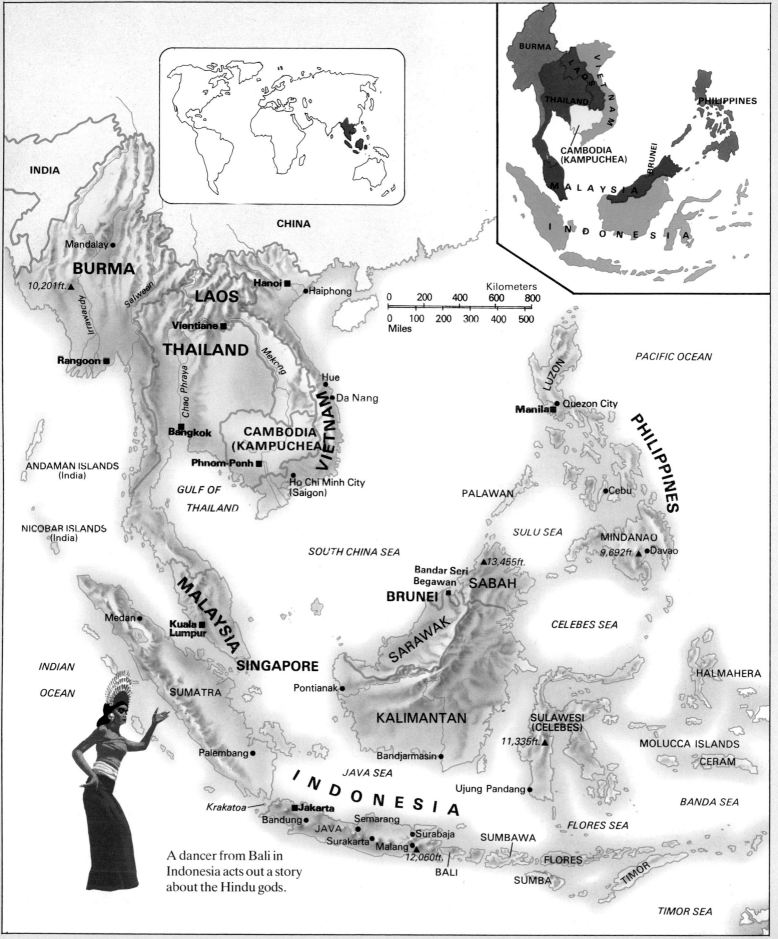

INDIA

BURMA

Mandalay •

10,201ft. ▲

Irrawaddy

Salween

CHINA

LAOS

Hanoi ■

• Haiphong

Vientiane ■

THAILAND

Mekong

Rangoon ■

Chao Phraya

Hue

• Da Nang

VIETNAM

Bangkok ■

CAMBODIA
(KAMPUCHEA)

Phnom-Penh ■

• Ho Chi Minh City
(Saigon)

ANDAMAN ISLANDS
(India)

GULF OF
THAILAND

NICOBAR ISLANDS
(India)

Kilometers

| 0 | 200 | 400 | 600 | 800 |

| 0 | 100 | 200 | 300 | 400 | 500 |

Miles

PACIFIC OCEAN

LUZON

Manila ■ • Quezon City

PHILIPPINES

PALAWAN

• Cebu

SULU SEA

MINDANAO

9,692ft ▲ • Davao

▲13,455ft.

Bandar Seri
Begawan

SABAH

BRUNEI ■

CELEBES SEA

SOUTH CHINA SEA

MALAYSIA

Medan •

Kuala
Lumpur ■

SINGAPORE

SUMATRA

INDIAN
OCEAN

Pontianak •

SARAWAK

KALIMANTAN

Bandjarmasin •

HALMAHERA

SULAWESI
(CELEBES)

11,335ft. ▲

MOLUCCA ISLANDS

CERAM

Palembang •

JAVA SEA

Ujung Pandang •

BANDA SEA

Krakatoa

INDONESIA

■ Jakarta

Bandung •

JAVA

Semarang

Surabaja •

Surakarta •

Malang •

12,060ft. ▲

BALI

SUMBAWA

FLORES SEA

FLORES

SUMBA

TIMOR

TIMOR SEA

A dancer from Bali in
Indonesia acts out a story
about the Hindu gods.

BURMA

LAOS

VIETNAM

THAILAND

CAMBODIA
(KAMPUCHEA)

PHILIPPINES

BRUNEI

MALAYSIA

INDONESIA

Canada

Canada is the second-largest country in the world. Only the U.S.S.R. is larger. Vast areas in the far north are uninhabited and only a small number of trappers and fishermen live in the snow-blanketed forests around the Hudson Bay.

Most Canadians live in the south, not far from the United States border, where the climate is warmer. The Prairie Provinces of Manitoba, Saskatchewan, and Alberta lie west of the Great Lakes. Sometimes they are called the "food basket of the world" because wheat farms stretch as far as the eye can see.

Canada's original people arrived there over 20,000 years ago. They came from Asia and their descendants today are the North American Indians and the Inuit (Eskimos). British and French settlers did not arrive until the seventeenth century.

Large deposits of minerals as well as fertile plains and rich forests help make Canada one of the wealthiest countries in the world. Canadians are proud too of their beautiful lakes and mountains and the cool, clean air of their forests.

Left: Lake Moraine is high in the Rockies in Banff National Park, Alberta.

QUEEN ELIZABETH ISLANDS

MELVILLE I.

DEVON I.

BAFFIN BAY

VICTORIA
ISLAND

BAFFIN ISLAND

ATLANTIC OCEAN

WEST TERRITORIES

HUDSON STRAIT

lave Lake

Lake
Athabasca

HUDSON BAY

NEWFOUNDLAND

Churchill

Churchill

Nelson

LABRADOR

ATCHEWAN

MANITOBA

QUEBEC

St John's

Saskatchewan

Albany

Saskatoon

Lake
Winnipeg

Fort Rupert

PRINCE
EDWARD I

gina

ONTARIO

St Lawrence

Charlottetown

Winnipeg

Kenora

Lake
Nipigon

Quebec

Fredericton

NEW
BRUNSWICK

Brandon

Lake Superior

Trois Rivieres

Halifax

NOVA SCOTIA

Sudbury

Montreal

Ottawa

Lake Huron

Lake Michigan

Toronto

Lake
Ontario

Hamilton

Niagara Falls

Lake Erie

Top: Niagara Falls is on the border of
Canada and the United States.
Above: Eskimo children build an igloo
in Labrador.

Left: Cattle graze
on the foothills of
the Rockies. East of
the mountains,
prairies and forests
stretch all the way
across the country
to the Great Lakes.

Kilometers

| 0 | 200 | 400 | 600 | 800 |

| 0 | 100 | 200 | 300 | 400 | 500 |
Miles

★ = provincial capital

47

United States

The United States of America is the fourth-largest country in the world and has the fourth-largest population and land area. It is divided into fifty states and includes Alaska in the northwest and Hawaii, a group of islands in the Pacific Ocean.

Like Canada, the United States was first settled by Indians whose ancestors came from Asia. In the eighteenth and nineteenth centuries, large numbers of settlers came to the "New World" from Europe in search of a better way of life. These people first settled on the East Coast and started the first thirteen states. Blacks were brought over from Africa to work on the plantations. Gradually people with pioneering

Above: Yavapai Point, in Grand Canyon National Park, Arizona. The Canyon was formed by the Colorado River.

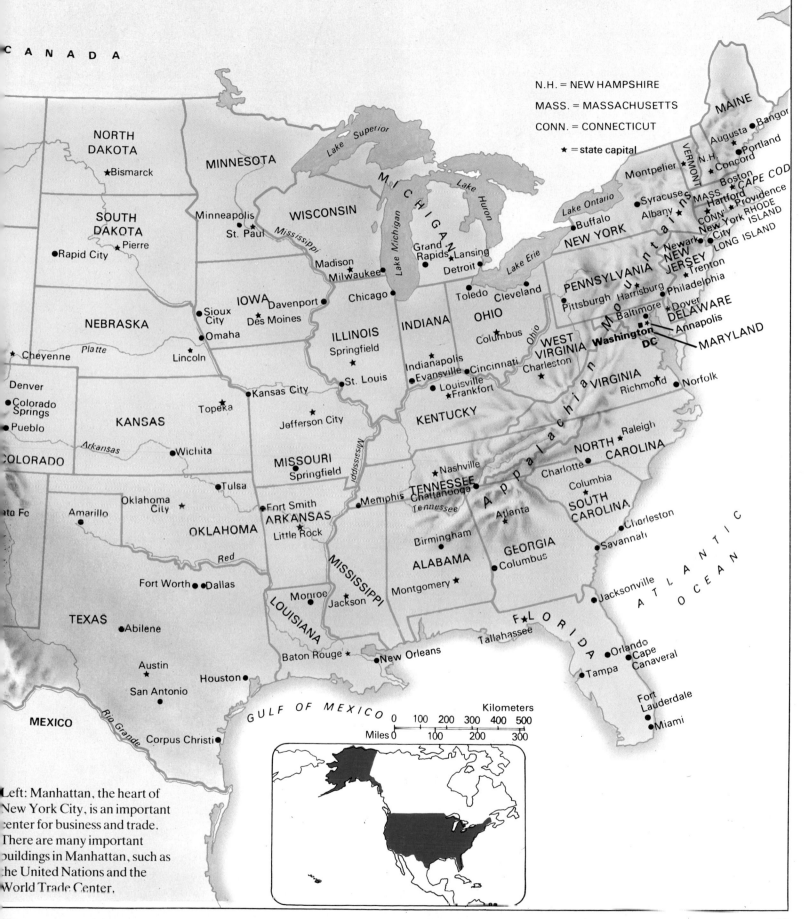

CANADA

NORTH DAKOTA
★Bismarck

MINNESOTA

Lake Superior

MICHIGAN

MAINE
Augusta ● Bangor
N.H. Portland
★ Concord

N.H. = NEW HAMPSHIRE
MASS. = MASSACHUSETTS
CONN. = CONNECTICUT
★ = state capital

VERMONT
Montpelier ★
Lake Huron
Lake Ontario
Syracuse
Buffalo
Albany ★

CAPE COD
Boston ★
MASS. Hartford★ ●Providence
CONN. ★ RHODE
New York ISLAND
City LONG ISLAND

SOUTH DAKOTA
●Rapid City ★Pierre

Minneapolis ●
St. Paul ★
Mississippi

WISCONSIN

Lake Michigan

Grand Rapids ● ★Lansing
Detroit

Madison ★
Milwaukee ●

IOWA
●Davenport
Sioux City ●
Des Moines ★

Chicago ●

Toledo ● Cleveland ●
Lake Erie

NEW YORK

PENNSYLVANIA
Pittsburgh ● Harrisburg ★
Ohio

Newark ●
NEW JERSEY ★Trenton
Philadelphia ●
Baltimore ● Dover ★
DELAWARE
Washington ★ Annapolis
DC MARYLAND

NEBRASKA
● Cheyenne
Omaha ●
Platte
Lincoln ★

OHIO
Columbus ★

INDIANA
Indianapolis ★
Evansville ● Cincinnati ●
Louisville ●
Frankfort ★

WEST VIRGINIA
Charleston ★

Denver ●
● Colorado Springs
● Pueblo

COLORADO

ILLINOIS
Springfield ★
St. Louis ★

Kansas City ●
Topeka ★

KANSAS
Arkansas
Wichita ●

Jefferson City ★

MISSOURI
Springfield ●

KENTUCKY

VIRGINIA
Richmond ★ ● Norfolk

Appalachian Mountains

NORTH CAROLINA
Raleigh ★

Santa Fe
Amarillo ●

Tulsa ●

Oklahoma City ★

OKLAHOMA

Fort Smith ●
ARKANSAS
Little Rock ★

Nashville ★
Chattanooga ●
Memphis ●
Tennessee

TENNESSEE

Charlotte ●
Columbia ★

SOUTH CAROLINA
Charleston ●

Fort Worth ● ●Dallas
Red

Monroe ●
Jackson ★
MISSISSIPPI

Birmingham ●

ALABAMA
Montgomery ★

Columbus ●
GEORGIA

Savannah ●

Jacksonville ●

ATLANTIC OCEAN

TEXAS
● Abilene

Austin ★
San Antonio ●

Houston ●

LOUISIANA
Baton Rouge ★ ● New Orleans

Tallahassee ★
FLORIDA

Orlando ●
Tampa ●
Cape Canaveral ●

MEXICO

Rio Grande

Corpus Christi ●

GULF OF MEXICO

Kilometers
0 100 200 300 400 500
Miles 0   100   200   300

Fort Lauderdale ●
● Miami

Left: Manhattan, the heart of
New York City, is an important
center for business and trade.
There are many important
buildings in Manhattan, such as
the United Nations and the
World Trade Center.

spirits ventured westward and new states were formed. Some farmed on the Midwestern plains while explorers and miners traveled through the Rocky Mountains to the Pacific coast. Today people from all over the world live in the United States.

Like their Canadian neighbors, most Americans have a high standard of living. The United States is an extremely wealthy country. It has large resources of oil, gas, coal, and many metals, huge farms and plantations and more factories than any other country in the world.

Above right: Las Vegas, Nevada, is famous for gambling and nightclubs.

Right: This view of the Delaware River shows the rich growth and beauty of the New Jersey region.

Left: Oil drilling is a common sight in Texas.

Below: The government of the United States includes the Senate and the House of Representatives. They meet in the Capitol building in Washington D.C.

Baseball is one of the most popular sports in the United States.

Eastern and Southern States

State	Popular name	Capital	Bird	Flower	Tree
Alabama	Yellowhammer State	Montgomery	Yellowhammer	Camellia	Southern pine (Longleaf pine)
Arkansas	Land of Opportunity	Little Rock	Mockingbird	Apple blossom	Pine
Connecticut	Constitution State	Hartford	Robin	Mountain laurel	White oak
Delaware	First State	Dover	Blue hen chicken	Peach blossom	American holly
Florida	Sunshine State	Tallahassee	Mockingbird	Orange blossom	Cabbage palm
Georgia	Empire State of the South	Atlanta	Brown thrasher	Cherokee rose	Live oak
Kentucky	Bluegrass State	Frankfort	Cardinal	Goldenrod	Tulip poplar
Louisiana	Pelican State	Baton Rouge	Brown pelican	Magnolia	Bald cypress
Maine	Pine Tree State	Augusta	Chickadee	White pine cone and tassel	White pine
Maryland	Old Line State	Annapolis	Baltimore oriole	Black-eyed Susan	White oak
Massachusetts	Bay State	Boston	Chickadee	Arbutus (Mayflower)	American elm
Mississippi	Magnolia State	Jackson	Mockingbird	Magnolia	Magnolia
New Hampshire	Granite State	Concord	Purple finch	Purple lilac	White birch
New Jersey	Garden State	Trenton	Eastern goldfinch	Purple violet	Red oak
New York	Empire State	Albany	Bluebird	Rose	Sugar maple
North Carolina	Tar Heel State	Raleigh	Cardinal	Flowering dogwood	Pine
Oklahoma	Sooner State	Oklahoma City	Scissor-tailed flycatcher	Mistletoe	Redbud
Pennsylvania	Keystone State	Harrisburg	Ruffed grouse	Mountain laurel	Hemlock
Rhode Island	Little Rhody	Providence	Rhode Island Red	Violet	Red maple
South Carolina	Palmetto State	Columbia	Carolina wren	Carolina jessamine	Palmetto
Tennessee	Volunteer State	Nashville	Mockingbird	Iris	Tulip poplar
Texas	Lone Star State	Austin	Mockingbird	Bluebonnet	Pecan
Vermont	Green Mountain State	Montpelier	Hermit thrush	Red clover	Sugar maple
Virginia	Old Dominion	Richmond	Cardinal	Flowering dogwood	none
West Virginia	Mountain State	Charleston	Cardinal	Rhododendron	Sugar maple

This small church among trees turning color is typical of the scenic Vermont countryside.

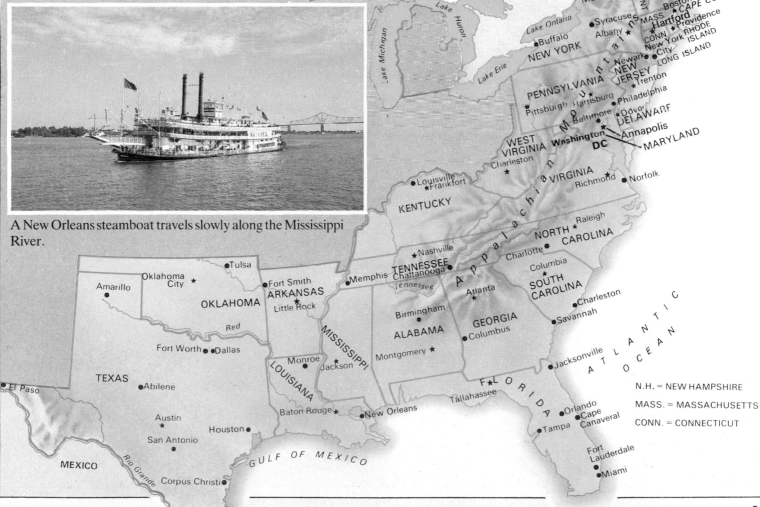

A New Orleans steamboat travels slowly along the Mississippi River.

N.H. = NEW HAMPSHIRE

MASS. = MASSACHUSETTS

CONN. = CONNECTICUT

The Midwest

State	Popular name	Capital	Bird	Flower	Tree
Illinois	Land of Lincoln	Springfield	Cardinal	Native violet	White oak
Indiana	Hoosier State	Indianapolis	Cardinal	Peony	Tulip tree or Yellow poplar
Iowa	Hawkeye State	Des Moines	Eastern goldfinch	Wild rose	Oak
Kansas	Sunflower State	Topeka	Western meadow lark	Sunflower	Cottonwood
Michigan	Wolverine State	Lansing	Robin	Apple blossom	White pine
Minnesota	Gopher State	St. Paul	Common loon	Pink and white lady's slipper	Norway or red pine
Missouri	Show Me State	Jefferson City	Bluebird	Hawthorn	Flowering dogwood
Nebraska	Cornhusker State	Lincoln	Western meadow lark	Goldenrod	American elm
North Dakota	Flickertail State	Bismarck	Western meadow lark	Wild prairie rose	American elm
Ohio	Buckeye State	Columbus	Cardinal	Scarlet carnation	Buckeye
South Dakota	Sunshine State	Pierre	Ring-necked pheasant	American pasque-flower	Black Hills spruce
Wisconsin	Badger State	Madison	Robin	Wood violet	Sugar maple

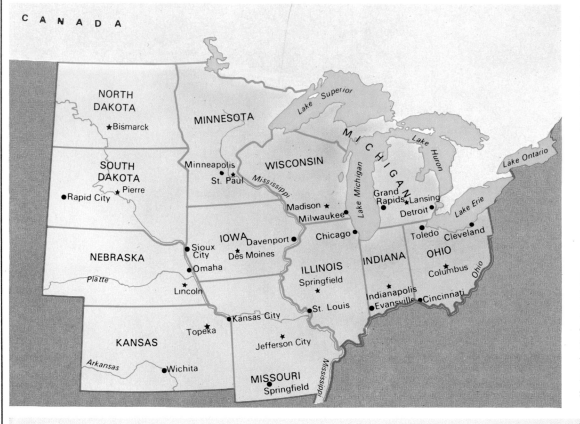

Automobile manufacturing is a very important industry in Detroit, Michigan. The industry provides jobs for many people. Car and truck parts are made and then they are assembled. This assembly line is at the Ford Motor Company.

Huge fields of soybeans have been planted on this farm in Iowa. Most of the midwest is covered by farmland. Other important crops are corn, wheat, tobacco, and maize. In addition, cattle, pigs, and sheep are often raised.

Western and Mountain States

State	Popular name	Capital	Bird	Flower	Tree
Alaska	Last Frontier	Juneau	Willow ptarmigan	Forget-me-not	Sitka spruce
Arizona	Grand Canyon State	Phoenix	Cactus wren	Saguaro	Paloverde
California	Golden State	Sacramento	California valley quail	Golden poppy	California redwood
Colorado	Centennial State	Denver	Lark bunting	Rocky Mt. columbine	Blue spruce
Hawaii	Aloha State	Honolulu	Nene (Hawaiian goose)	Hibiscus	Kukui
Idaho	Gem State	Boise	Mountain bluebird	Syringa (Mock orange)	Western white pine
Montana	Treasure State	Helena	Western meadow lark	Bitterroot	Ponderosa pine
Nevada	Silver State	Carson City	Mountain bluebird	Sagebrush	Single-leaf pinon
New Mexico	Land of Enchantment	Santa Fe	Road runner	Yucca	Pinon or nut pine
Oregon	Beaver State	Salem	Western meadow lark	Oregon grape	Douglas fir
Utah	Beehive State	Salt Lake City	Seagull	Sego lily	Blue spruce
Washington	Evergreen State	Olympia	Willow goldfinch	Coast rhododendron	Western hemlock
Wyoming	Equality State	Cheyenne	Meadow lark	Indian paintbrush	Cottonwood

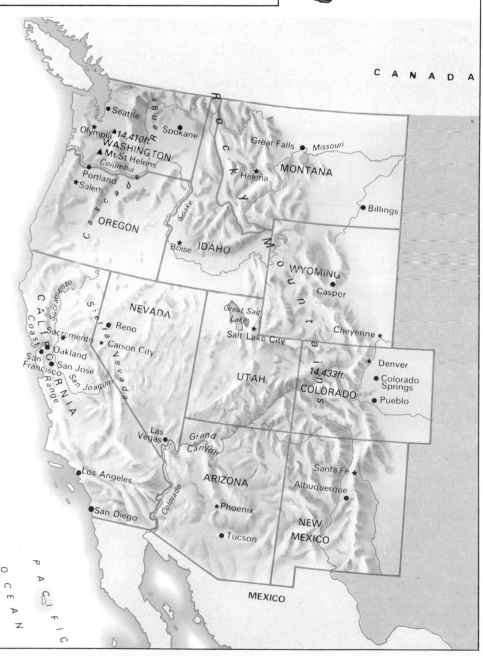

Right: You can meet Mickey and Minnie Mouse and other Walt Disney characters in Disneyland. Disneyland is in California and Disneyworld is in Florida.

Cable cars run on tracks up and down the hilly streets of San Francisco.

For location of Alaska and Hawaii see (map) page 49.

Central America and the

Antigua & Barbuda

Bahamas

Barbados

Cuba

Dominica

Dominican Republic

Grenada

St. Christopher Nevis

Haiti

Jamaica

St. Lucia

St.Vincent & Grenadines

Trinidad & Tobago

Mexico and seven small Central American countries make up the land link between the United States and South America.

The people living in Mexico, Central America and the islands of the West Indies are descendants either of the original people or of Europeans and blacks. Most of them speak Spanish, English, French, or American Indian languages. In 1492, when Christopher Columbus reached the islands in the Caribbean Sea, he thought he had sailed around the world to India. He called the people living there "Indians" and the islands were named the West Indies.

Central America and the thousands of West Indian islands are mostly hot and mountainous. The climate is ideal for growing fruit, coffee, cotton, tobacco, and sugarcane. Cuba is the largest of the West Indian islands and it is the third-largest producer of sugar in the world. Many of the islands are popular vacation places because of their sunny climate and easygoing atmosphere.

In Mexico most people work on small farms. The main crop is corn. A favorite meal is *tortillas*, a pancake made from corn flour. Gold and other metals are mined in Mexico, but the most important industry is oil.

Below left: The warm Caribbean Sea is ideal for sailing, swimming, and snorkeling.

Caribbean

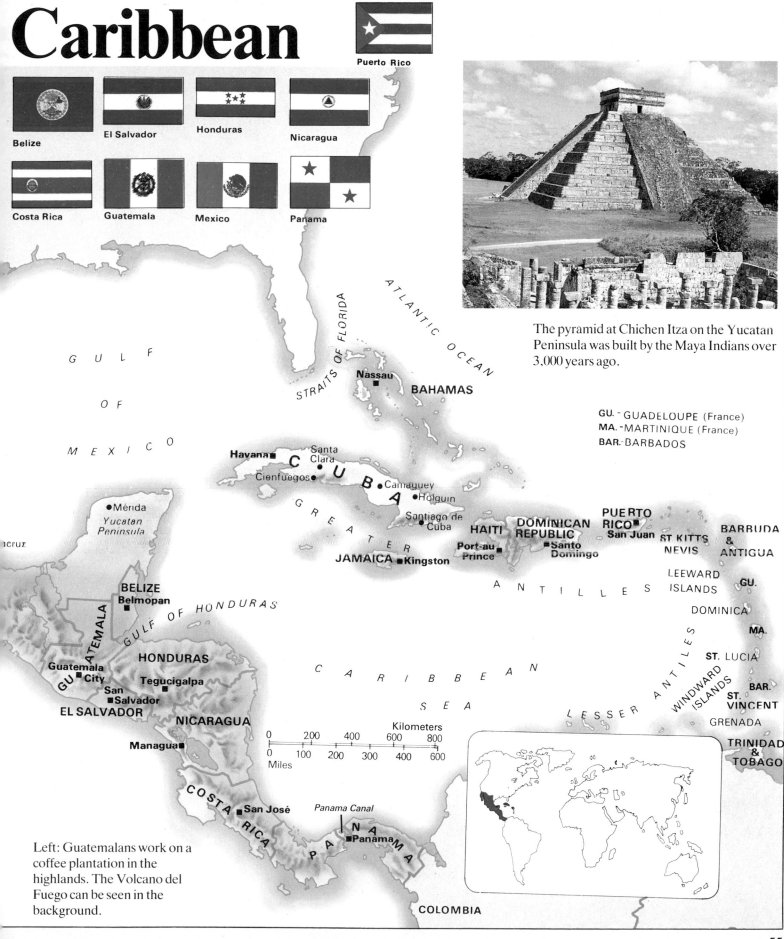

Puerto Rico

Belize

El Salvador

Honduras

Nicaragua

Costa Rica

Guatemala

Mexico

Panama

The pyramid at Chichen Itza on the Yucatan Peninsula was built by the Maya Indians over 3,000 years ago.

GU. - GUADELOUPE (France)
MA. - MARTINIQUE (France)
BAR. - BARBADOS

ATLANTIC OCEAN

STRAITS OF FLORIDA

GULF OF MEXICO

Nassau

BAHAMAS

Havana
Santa Clara
CUBA
Cienfuegos
Camaguey
Holguin
Santiago de Cuba

GREATER

Mérida
Yucatan Peninsula

cruz

HAITI
DOMINICAN REPUBLIC
PUERTO RICO
San Juan
ST KITTS NEVIS
BARBUDA & ANTIGUA

Port-au-Prince
Santo Domingo

JAMAICA
Kingston

ANTILLES

LEEWARD ISLANDS

GU.

DOMINICA

MA.

BELIZE
Belmopan

GULF OF HONDURAS

CARIBBEAN

SEA

ST. LUCIA

WINDWARD ISLANDS

BAR.

ST. VINCENT

GRENADA

GUATEMALA

Guatemala City
GU.
San Salvador

HONDURAS
Tegucigalpa

EL SALVADOR

NICARAGUA

Managua

LESSER ANTILLES

TRINIDAD & TOBAGO

Kilometers
0   200   400   600   800
0   100   200   300   400   600
Miles

San José

COSTA RICA

Panama Canal

PANAMA

Panama

Left: Guatemalans work on a coffee plantation in the highlands. The Volcano del Fuego can be seen in the background.

COLOMBIA

55

The Andean Countries

The Andes Mountains rise above much of Colombia, Ecuador, Peru, and Bolivia. They form high tablelands, or *plateaus*, where the climate is cool even though the equator passes through Ecuador and Colombia. Many rivers that feed the Amazon River begin in the Andes and travel eastward through thick tropical forests.

Bananas and coffee are grown on plantations where the climate is hot and tropical. As transport across the mountains gets better, more people are living in the Amazon lowlands. Here they farm and work in mines. But much of the land is covered by thick forest and cannot be farmed.

Over 800 years ago the Andes were populated by the Incas. Gold and silver in the mountains attracted the Spaniards, who eventually destroyed the Inca civilization. Today minerals are still important, especially in Bolivia. Spanish is the official language spoken in the Andean countries.

Colombia

Ecuador

Peru

Bolivia

Left: Llamas are herded in the Andes near Cuzco, Peru. Their wool is used to make warm clothing.

Below: Indians live in the interior of Colombia, far from the modern world. In this picture rice is pounded with a large mortar and pestles.

Above: Indians in colorful clothes gather in a market in Ecuador to sell their fruit and vegetables. Many Indians in the Andean countries still speak the old Indian languages: Quechua and Aymara.

Below: Traditional reed boats lie on the beaches of Lake Titicaca in Peru. Some Peruvians make their living by fishing in the lake and farming the surrounding land.

PANAMA

Cartagena
19,029ft.
Barranquilla

Medellin
Bucaramanga

VENEZUELA

GUYANA

Cali
Bogotá

COLOMBIA

18,865ft.

20,561ft. Quito
Guayaquil

ECUADOR

Iquitos

Amazon

BRAZIL

Piura
Maranon

Chiclayo
Trujillo
Chimbote
22,205ft.

PERU

Madeira

Callao Lima
Huancayo

Cuzco
20,945ft.
El Misti
19,101ft.
Arequipa
Lake Titicaca

Beni

BOLIVIA

La Paz
Cochabamba
Santa Cruz

Lake Poopo
Sucre

22,162ft.

CHILE

PARAGUAY

PACIFIC

OCEAN

22,572ft.

ARGENTINA

22,831ft.

Kilometers
0   200   400   600   800
0 100 200 300 400 500
Miles

57

Brazil and Its Neighbors

People of many different races live together in eastern South America. There are American Indians and *mestizos*, who are mixed Indian and European people. Other people are direct descendants of Europeans or Africans. Most of the early settlers were Spanish or Portuguese and most South Americans today speak one of these languages. Many people are also Roman Catholic.

Brazil is the largest country in South America. Much of the land is covered in thick Amazon rain forest. Most people live in big cities, such as Rio de Janeiro and Sao Paulo near the Atlantic coast. The northeastern part of Brazil is poorer. Land is owned by a few rich landlords who employ farmers. In bad years the farmers have to go to the cities in search of other work.

Brazil is famous for growing coffee. Sugar cane is also an important crop. Coal, iron ore, and other minerals are abundant in Brazil.

To the northeast of Brazil is Venezuela. Here rain forests also cover much of the land. Venezuela is a very rich country because it has valuable oil fields and iron ore. The money received from selling oil provides Venezuelans with factories, modern homes, and roads.

Guyana, Surinam, and French Guiana were once colonies of the British, Dutch, and French. In these countries most people live in cities along the coast.

Above: The Amazon River flows through the thick, hot jungle. It is part of the world's greatest river system.

Left: The Indians living in the Mato Grosso region of Brazil often wear traditional face paint.

Right: A huge statue of Christ watches over Corcovado Peak and the beautiful harbor of Rio de Janeiro. A lively carnival takes place in this city every year.

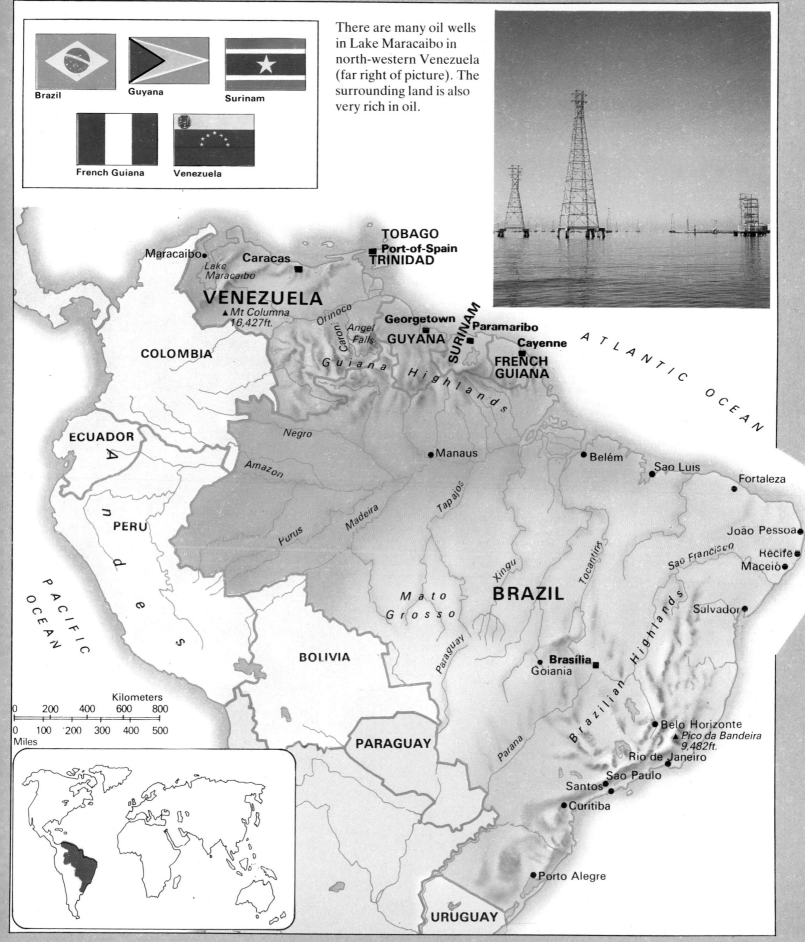

Brazil

Guyana

Surinam

French Guiana

Venezuela

There are many oil wells in Lake Maracaibo in north-western Venezuela (far right of picture). The surrounding land is also very rich in oil.

TOBAGO
Port-of-Spain
TRINIDAD

Maracaibo
Lake Maracaibo
Caracas
VENEZUELA
▲ Mt Columna 16,427ft.
Orinoco
Caroní
Angel Falls
Georgetown
GUYANA
SURINAM
Paramaribo
Cayenne
FRENCH GUIANA
Guiana Highlands
ATLANTIC OCEAN

COLOMBIA

ECUADOR

Negro

Amazon

Manaus

Belém

Sao Luis

Fortaleza

A n d e s

PERU

Purus

Madeira

Tapajos

João Pessoa

Recife

Maceió

Sao Francisco

PACIFIC OCEAN

Xingu

Mato Grosso

BRAZIL

Tocantins

Salvador

BOLIVIA

Paraguay

Brasília
Goiania

Brazilian Highlands

PARAGUAY

Parana

Belo Horizonte
▲ Pico da Bandeira 9,482ft.
Rio de Janeiro
Sao Paulo
Santos
Curitiba

Kilometers
0 200 400 600 800
0 100 200 300 400 500
Miles

Porto Alegre

URUGUAY

Southern South America

The countries of southern South America enjoy a mild climate, unlike their neighbors in the tropical north. The southern tip of the continent is very cool because it is not far from the frozen wastes of Antarctica.

Chile is long and narrow. In the north is the Atacama Desert, where workers mine copper and nitrate. Many people in Chile try to live off the land, but farming is hard in most areas. People are leaving their farms to work in cities such as Santiago and Valparaiso.

Argentina is the second-largest and the richest of all South American countries. Farmers rear sheep and cattle and grow wheat, sugar cane, and cotton on the fertile *pampas*, or grasslands. Factory workers in the cities process these products.

Most people living in Chile and Argentina are descendants of the Spanish and are Spanish-speaking. People from Europe, especially from Italy, still live in these countries today.

Argentina

Chile

Paraguay

Uruguay

Above: Patagonia is the name of the upland plain in the south of Argentina. There are oil, coal, and mineral deposits in this region.

Above left: Buenos Aires is the major port of Argentina.

Left: The copper mine at Chiquicamata in Chile is the largest open cast mine in the world.

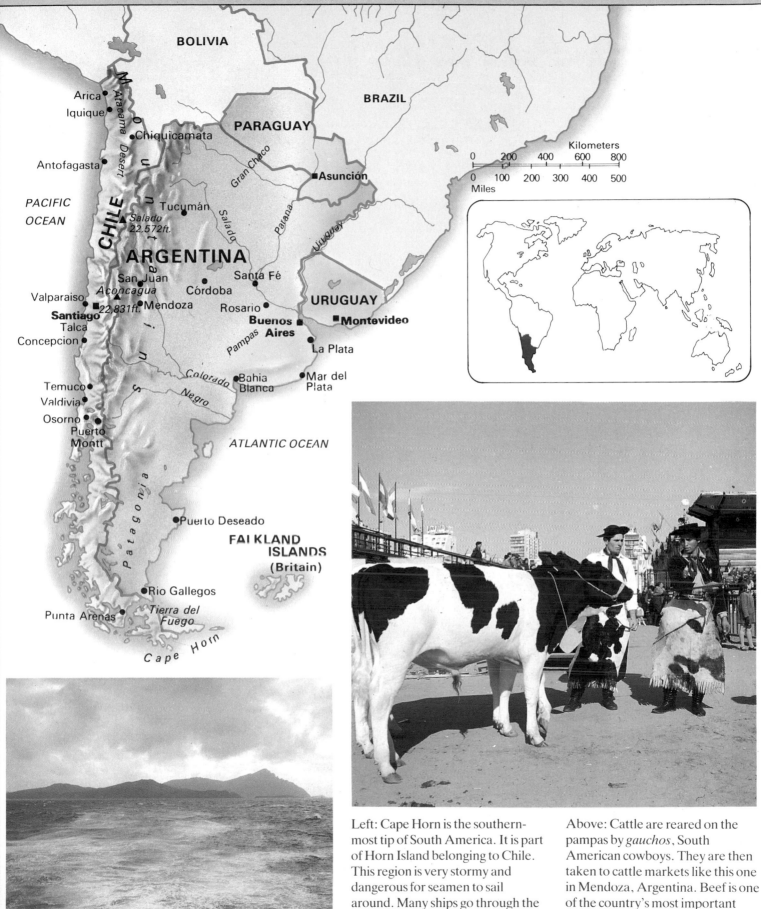

BOLIVIA

PARAGUAY

BRAZIL

Arica
Iquique
Chiquicamata
Antofagasta

Gran Chaco

Asunción

PACIFIC
OCEAN

CHILE

Atacama Desert

Tucumán
Salado
22,572ft.

ARGENTINA

Salado

Paraná

Uruguay

Mountains

San Juan
Aconcagua
22,831ft.

Córdoba
Mendoza

Santa Fé

Valparaiso
Santiago
Talca
Concepcion

Rosario

URUGUAY

Buenos
Aires

Montevideo

Pampas

La Plata

Colorado

Bahia
Blanca

Mar del
Plata

Temuco
Valdivia
Osorno
Puerto
Montt

Negro

Andes

ATLANTIC OCEAN

Patagonia

Puerto Deseado

FALKLAND
ISLANDS
(Britain)

Rio Gallegos

Punta Arenas

Tierra del
Fuego

Cape Horn

Kilometers
0 200 400 600 800
0 100 200 300 400 500
Miles

Left: Cape Horn is the southern-most tip of South America. It is part of Horn Island belonging to Chile. This region is very stormy and dangerous for seamen to sail around. Many ships go through the Panama Canal instead.

Above: Cattle are reared on the pampas by *gauchos*, South American cowboys. They are then taken to cattle markets like this one in Mendoza, Argentina. Beef is one of the country's most important exports.

North Africa

The vast Sahara Desert covers almost all of northern Africa. It is the largest, hottest desert in the world, stretching for 3,000 miles from the Atlantic Ocean to the Red Sea. In the northwest, in Morocco and Algeria, lie the rugged Atlas Mountains.

The people of northern Africa are mostly Muslim Arabs and Berbers who earn their living from farming. They live in river valleys and around oases because there is no water in other areas. In Egypt it scarcely ever rains, except along the Mediterranean coast. Most farmers rely on the river Nile for water. The Aswan Dam, built on the Nile, stores water for use during dry periods.

Tourists travel to Tunisia and Morocco to enjoy sunbathing on the beaches and wandering through the colorful bazaars. But many more tourists visit Egypt to see the pyramids at Giza—one of the Seven Wonders of the World.

Below: The pyramids at Giza were built to be the burial tombs for the kings of Ancient Egypt.
Below right: In Mali boats carry goods along the Niger River.
Far right: Flare stacks around a desert oil field in Libya.

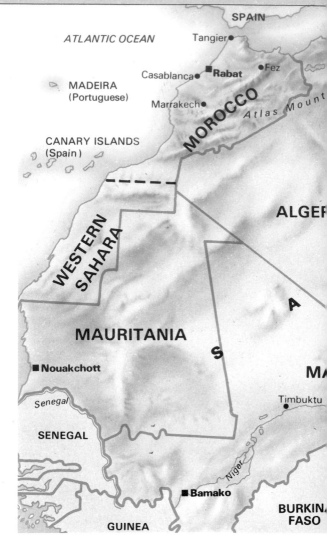

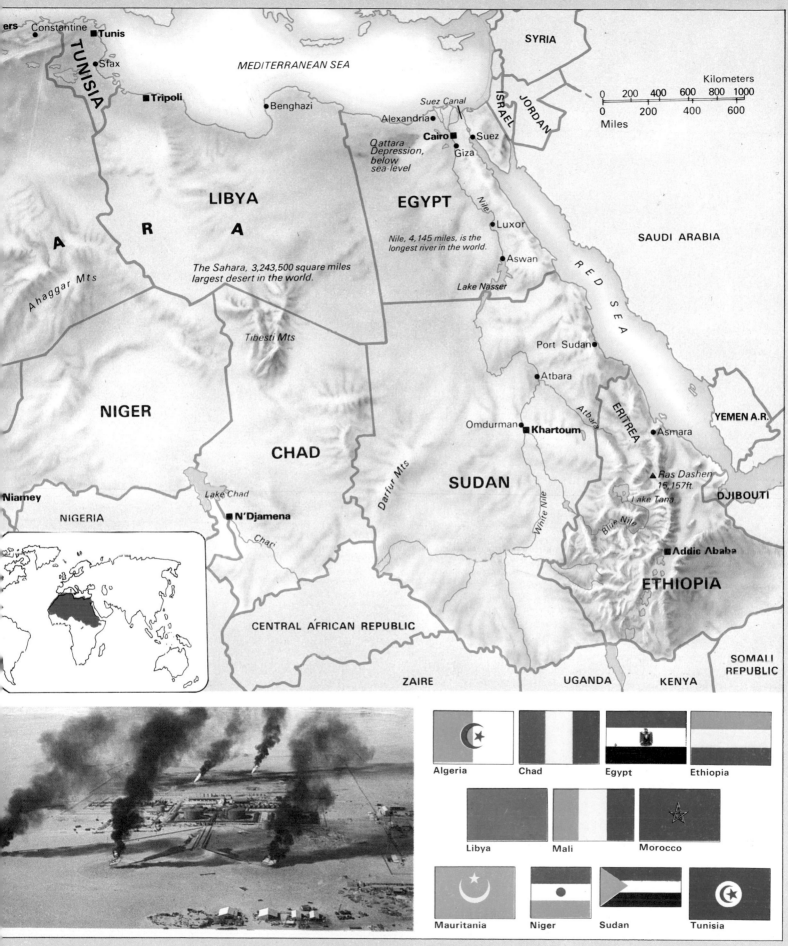

ers
Constantine ■**Tunis**
■**TUNISIA**
•Sfax

■**Tripoli**

MEDITERRANEAN SEA

•Benghazi

SYRIA

ISRAEL
JORDAN

Suez Canal
Alexandria•
Cairo ■ •Suez
Qattara Depression, below sea-level
Giza•

LIBYA

EGYPT

A R A

Nile

The Sahara, 3,243,500 square miles largest desert in the world.

Nile, 4,145 miles, is the longest river in the world.

•Luxor

•Aswan

Lake Nasser

RED SEA

SAUDI ARABIA

Kilometers
0 200 400 600 800 1000
0   200   400   600
Miles

Ahaggar Mts

Tibesti Mts

NIGER

Port Sudan•

•Atbara

Atbara

ERITREA
•Asmara

YEMEN A.R.

CHAD

Omdurman• ■**Khartoum**

Darfur Mts

SUDAN

▲*Ras Dashen 15,157ft.*
Lake Tana

DJIBOUTI

•Niamey

Lake Chad

White Nile

Blue Nile

NIGERIA

■**N'Djamena**

Chari

■**Addis Ababa**

ETHIOPIA

CENTRAL AFRICAN REPUBLIC

SOMALI REPUBLIC

ZAIRE

UGANDA

KENYA

Algeria

Chad

Egypt

Ethiopia

Libya

Mali

Morocco

Mauritania

Niger

Sudan

Tunisia

West Africa

West Africa is a jigsaw puzzle of countries. Many different groups of black Africans live there. Nigeria alone has 250 groups. The people speak a number of African languages, including Swahili. But official languages are often English, French, or Portuguese because most of these countries were once ruled by these European nations.

The countries along the coast are hot and have long, wet seasons. They are largely covered by tropical forest. Cocoa, coffee, palm oil, and rubber are important crops. Root crops of cassava and yams provide food. Farther inland, on savanna grasslands, crops consist of cotton and groundnuts. Millet, corn, and sorghum are grown for food. Cattle are kept for their meat, as well as for their hides and skins.

West African countries are building up their industries. There are new factories in Nigeria and Senegal, metals are mined in Sierra Leone and Ghana, and oil is drilled in Nigeria.

Crops and minerals are exported and the money received from selling these products is used to build modern towns, schools, and hospitals. But many of the people still live on the land in the same way as their families have lived for centuries. Some live in clearings in the hot forests and work small gardens. Others herd animals on the *savanna* grasslands.

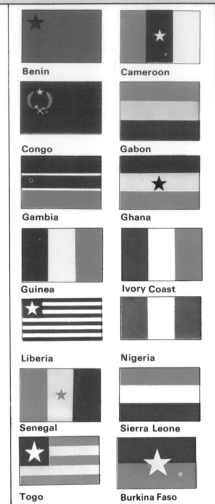

Benin Cameroon Congo Gabon Gambia Ghana Guinea Ivory Coast Liberia Nigeria Senegal Sierra Leone Togo Burkina Faso

Left: A Nigerian woman in colorful dress stands in the center of Lagos, the modern capital of Nigeria.

Below: Cocoa trees grow on large plantations in Ghana. Their huge pods are cut off with large knives. The beans inside are then dried and used to make chocolate and cocoa.

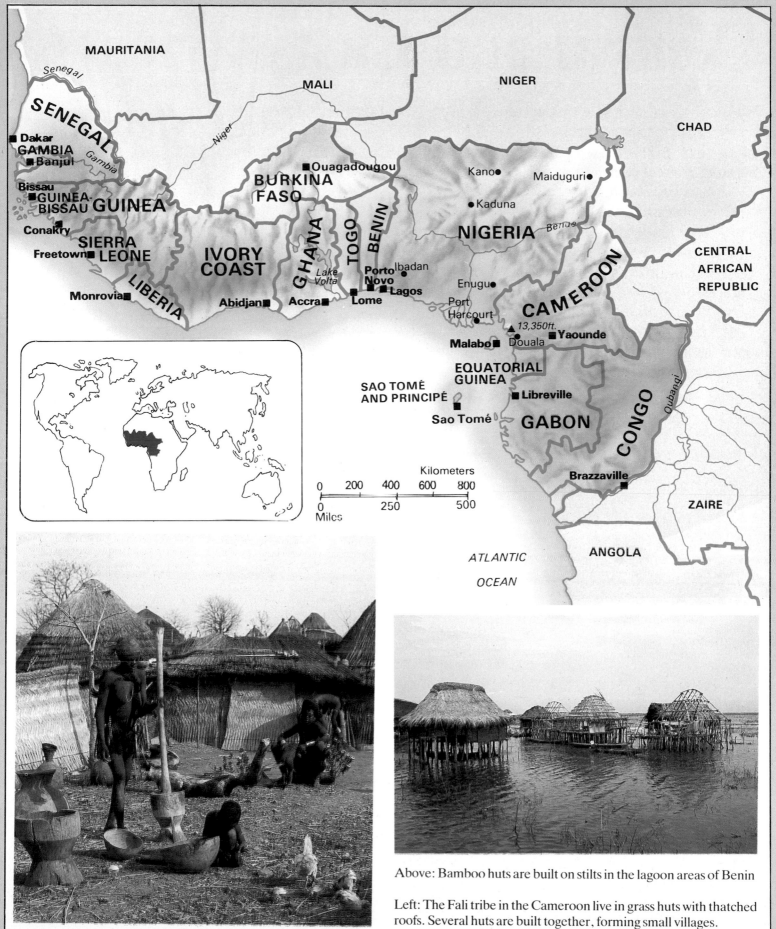

MAURITANIA

Senegal

MALI

NIGER

CHAD

SENEGAL

■ Dakar
GAMBIA
■ Banjul

Niger

Gambia

Bissau
GUINEA-
BISSAU GUINEA

Conakry

SIERRA
LEONE
Freetown ■

Monrovia ■

IVORY
COAST

LIBERIA

BURKINA
FASO

■ Ouagadougou

GHANA

TOGO

BENIN

Abidjan ■

Accra ■

Lome ■

Porto
Novo ■
Lagos ■

Lake
Volta

Kano ●

● Kaduna

Ibadan

Enugu ●

NIGERIA

Benue

Maiduguri ●

CAMEROON

CENTRAL
AFRICAN
REPUBLIC

Port
Harcourt ●

▲ 13,350ft.

Malabo ■

Douala ■

■ Yaounde

EQUATORIAL
GUINEA

SAO TOMÉ
AND PRINCIPÉ ■

■ Libreville

Sao Tomé ■

GABON

CONGO

Oubangi

Kilometers

0   200   400   600   800

0   250   500
Miles

Brazzaville ■

ZAIRE

ATLANTIC

OCEAN

ANGOLA

Above: Bamboo huts are built on stilts in the lagoon areas of Benin

Left: The Fali tribe in the Cameroon live in grass huts with thatched roofs. Several huts are built together, forming small villages.

Central and East Africa

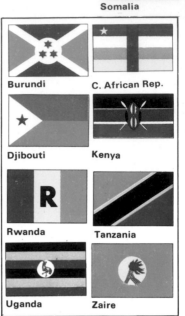

Somalia

Burundi   C. African Rep.

Djibouti   Kenya

R

Rwanda   Tanzania

Uganda   Zaire

Much of Central Africa is lowland covered with thick tropical forest. One of the greatest rivers in Africa, the river Zaire, runs through the region and is important for transport. Most people in Central Africa live in small clearings, growing food crops such as yams and cassava. Sometimes parts of the forest are cleared for timber. Cocoa, coffee, palm oil, and rubber are also important. Zaire's main source of wealth comes from copper mines in the southeastern part of the country.

East Africa is a region of highland and *savanna* grassland. A cool climate is typical of the East African plateau. In the past Europeans settled in this area, growing tea, coffee, cotton, and sisal. Food crops consist of millet, corn, and plantains.

Tourists often travel to Kenya to see wild animals. Once hunted, many lions, elephants, zebras, and rhinos now live on large game reserves.

Somalia and Djibouti are mostly desert. The people living in these countries are animal herders and are often very poor.

The Bambuti, a tribe of pygmies, live in the forests of Zaire. They are the world's smallest people. They hunt game with spears, bows and arrows, and fish with nets.

An elephant herd grazes on the grasslands of Kenya. Behind them is Mount Kilimanjaro, the highest peak in Africa.

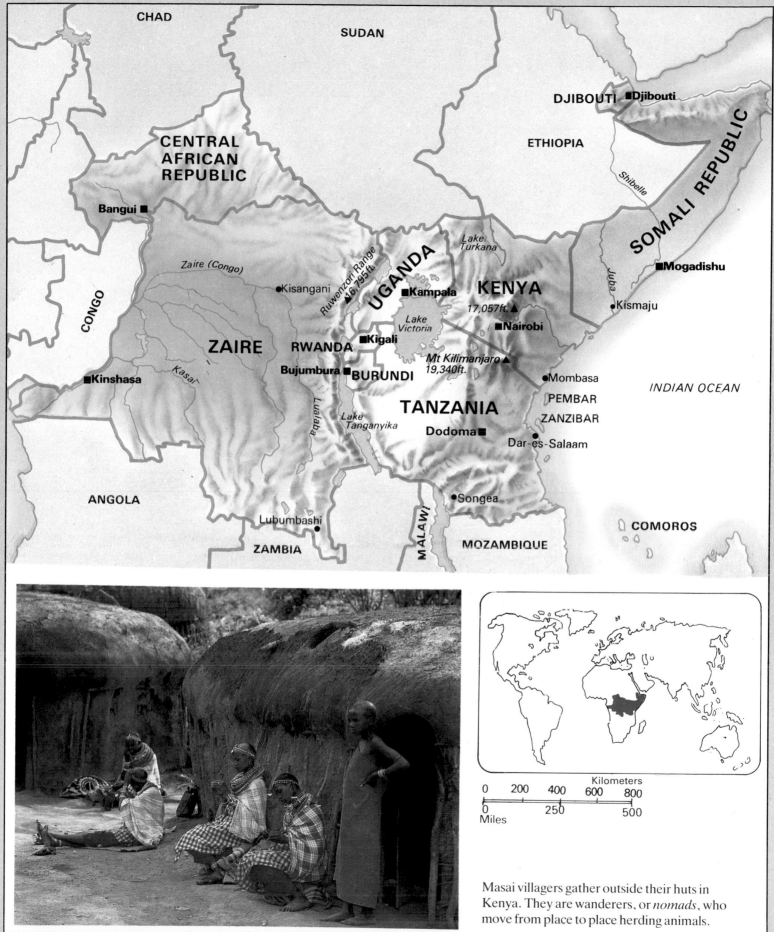

CHAD

SUDAN

DJIBOUTI ■Djibouti

ETHIOPIA

SOMALI REPUBLIC

CENTRAL
AFRICAN
REPUBLIC

Shibelle

Bangui ■

■Mogadishu

Zaire (Congo)

Ruwenzori Range
16,795ft.▲

*Lake
Turkana*

UGANDA

•Kisangani

■Kampala

KENYA

Juba

•Kismaju

CONGO

17,057ft.▲

ZAIRE

RWANDA

■Kigali

*Lake
Victoria*

/■Nairobi

■Kinshasa

Kasai

Bujumbura ■ ■BURUNDI

Mt Kilimanjaro
19,340ft.▲

•Mombasa

INDIAN OCEAN

PEMBAR

Lualaba

*Lake
Tanganyika*

TANZANIA

ZANZIBAR

ANGOLA

Dodoma ■

•Dar-es-Salaam

•Songea

Lubumbashi

◊ COMOROS

MALAWI

ZAMBIA

MOZAMBIQUE

Kilometers
0   200   400   600   800

0   250   500
Miles

Masai villagers gather outside their huts in
Kenya. They are wanderers, or *nomads*, who
move from place to place herding animals.

Southern Africa

Southern Africa is very different from the rest of Africa. To start with, its climate is cooler than the rest of Africa. Look for the Namib and Kalahari deserts on the map. Unlike the almost barren Sahara in northern Africa, the Kalahari is a dry, bush-covered plateau.

Many Europeans also live in this part of Africa. Large numbers of them first arrived in South Africa during the 1880s, attracted by the discovery of gold. Many stayed to farm the land or run mines and businesses.

South Africa and Zimbabwe are the richest countries in southern Africa. People from poorer countries, such as Botswana and Lesotho, often go to work in their large manufacturing industries. South Africa produces a huge share of the world's gold and diamonds. In Zimbabwe there are large cattle ranches as well as corn, cotton, and tobacco farms.

In South Africa there is a government policy called *apartheid* to keep Europeans and black Africans apart. Europeans control the government and own the major businesses. Madagascar is one of the largest islands in the world. Most people are farmers.

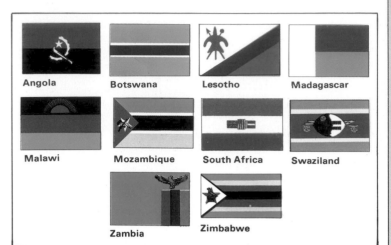

Angola Botswana Lesotho Madagascar

Malawi Mozambique South Africa Swaziland

Zambia Zimbabwe

Above: Lake Kariba is on the border of Zimbabwe and Zambia. The Kariba Dam in Zimbabwe provides water for the dry season.

Left: Gold is found in rock called *ore*. The ore is heated to melt the gold. This man is pouring gold into ingots.

Right: A Zulu woman wears her festival headdress. The Zulus are the largest group of black Africans in South Africa.

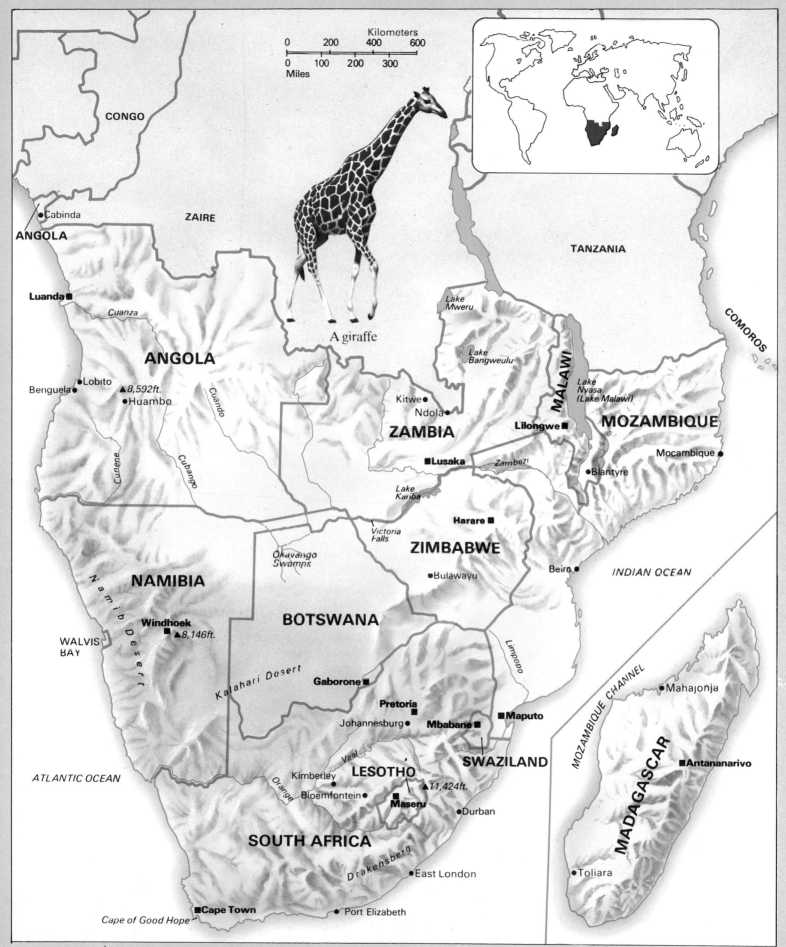

A giraffe

CONGO

ZAIRE

•Cabinda

ANGOLA

TANZANIA

COMOROS

Lake
Mweru

Luanda ■

Cuanza

ANGOLA

Benguela• •Lobito
▲8,592ft.
•Huambo

Cuando

Cubango

Cunene

Lake
Bangweulu

Kitwe•
Ndola•

ZAMBIA

■**Lusaka**

Lake
Nyasa
(Lake Malawi)

MALAWI

Lilongwe ■

MOZAMBIQUE

Mocambique•

•Blantyre

Zambezi

Lake
Kariba

Victoria
Falls

Harare ■

ZIMBABWE

Beira•

INDIAN OCEAN

Okavango
Swamps

•Bulawayo

N a m i b   D e s e r t

NAMIBIA

BOTSWANA

WALVIS
BAY

Windhoek
■ ▲8,146ft.

Kalahari Desert

Gaborone ■

Limpopo

MADAGASCAR

MOZAMBIQUE CHANNEL

•Mahajonja

ATLANTIC OCEAN

Pretoria
■
Johannesburg•

Mbabane ■

■**Maputo**

■**Antananarivo**

SWAZILAND

Kimberley•
Vaal

Orange

LESOTHO

Bloemfontein•

▲11,424ft.

Maseru

•Durban

•Toliara

SOUTH AFRICA

Drakensberg

•East London

■**Cape Town**

Cape of Good Hope

•Port Elizabeth

Kilometers
0   200   400   600
0 100 200 300
Miles

69

Australia

Australia is the smallest continent in the world. It is sometimes called "Down Under" because it lies south of the Equator among a group of islands in the Indian and Pacific Oceans.

Australia was discovered by Dutch sailors in the early 1600s. Much later, in 1770, Captain Cook took possession of parts of eastern Australia for Britain. At that time the Aborigines were the only people living there. Later, in the 1850s, gold was discovered and large numbers of settlers arrived from Europe in a hurry to make their fortunes. Today, besides gold, there are silver, copper, iron, zinc, and aluminum mines.

Much of the west of Australia is desert. Although it is a big country, it is not very crowded. Most people live in cities along the cooler southeast coast. In the dry, central plains called the "Outback," there are sheep and cattle stations. Sheep are kept mainly for their wool, which is sold to several other countries.

The Sydney opera house was built to look like the sailboats in the harbor. Sydney is the largest city in Australia.

A koala

Left: Ayers Rock rises high above the flat desert in the Northern Territory.

Below: Sheep stations cover much of the land west of the Great Dividing Range. These merino sheep are raised for their wool.

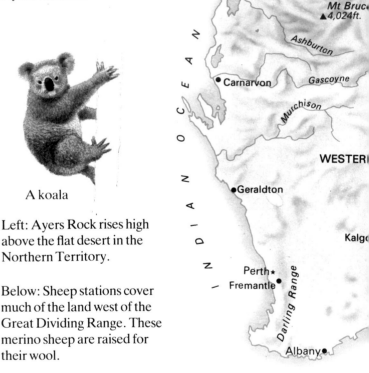

Port Hedland
Dampier
Mt Bruce
▲4,024ft.
Ashburton
Carnarvon
Gascoyne
Murchison
WESTER
Geraldton
Kalg
Perth★
Fremantle
Darling Range
Albany
INDIAN OCEAN

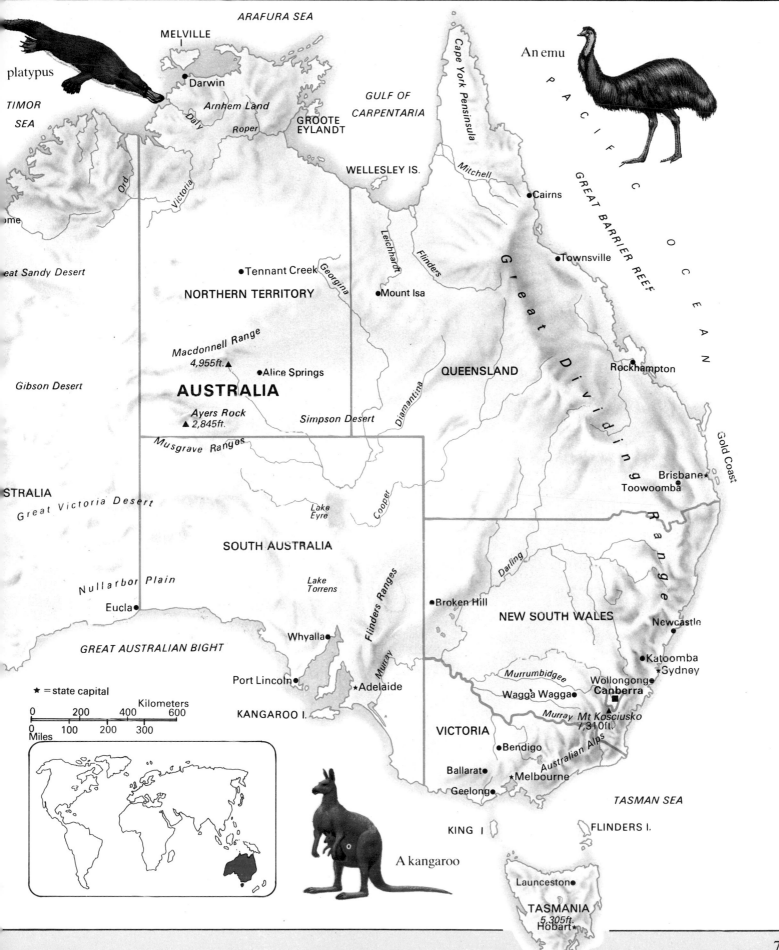

platypus

An emu

ARAFURA SEA

TIMOR SEA

MELVILLE I.

Darwin

Arnhem Land

Daly

Roper

GROOTE EYLANDT

GULF OF CARPENTARIA

Cape York Pensinsula

Ord

Victoria

Great Sandy Desert

WELLESLEY IS.

Mitchell

Leichhardt

Flinders

PACIFIC

GREAT BARRIER REEF

Cairns

Townsville

OCEAN

Tennant Creek

Georgina

NORTHERN TERRITORY

Mount Isa

Macdonnell Range 4,955ft.▲

Alice Springs

AUSTRALIA

Gibson Desert

QUEENSLAND

Rockhampton

Great Dividing

Ayers Rock ▲ 2,845ft.

Simpson Desert

Diamantina

STRALIA

Musgrave Ranges

Great Victoria Desert

Lake Eyre

Cooper

Gold Coast

Brisbane ★
Toowoomba

SOUTH AUSTRALIA

Nullarbor Plain

Lake Torrens

Eucla

GREAT AUSTRALIAN BIGHT

Whyalla

Flinders Ranges

Darling

Broken Hill

NEW SOUTH WALES

Newcastle

Range

Katoomba
★Sydney

Port Lincoln

Adelaide ★

Murrumbidgee

Wollongong
Canberra ▪

Murray

★ = state capital

Kilometers
0   200   400   600

Miles
0   100   200   300

KANGAROO I.

Wagga Wagga

Murray Mt Kosciusko
7,310ft.

VICTORIA

Australian Alps

Bendigo

Ballarat●

★Melbourne

Geelong●

TASMAN SEA

KING I.

FLINDERS I.

A kangaroo

Launceston●

TASMANIA
5,305ft.
Hobart★

New Zealand and the Pacific

New Zealand and the islands of the Pacific Ocean are divided into three groups—Melanesia, Micronesia, and Polynesia—according to the type of people who live on the islands. Kiribati and the Caroline islands form part of Micronesia, but Fiji and Papua New Guinea are included in Melanesia.

New Zealand is part of Polynesia because the Maoris, the original inhabitants, are Polynesian people. New Zealand has two main islands, North Island and South Island. In the 1800s settlers arrived from Britain to farm and to prospect for gold. Today most people live in towns and cities and the largest city is Auckland. But New Zealand remains a rich farming country. Dairy farming is very important and there are over 9 million cattle and 55 million sheep. Many factory workers process meat, butter, cheese, and milk.

Life on the Pacific Islands is often relaxed and simple. Many islanders live in small villages. They grow food in gardens and fish skillfully from canoes. Others on larger islands work on banana, coconut, and cocoa plantations. Few islands have mineral resources, but phosphates are mined on Nauru and there are copper mines on Bougainville, one of the tiny islands that belongs to Papua New Guinea.

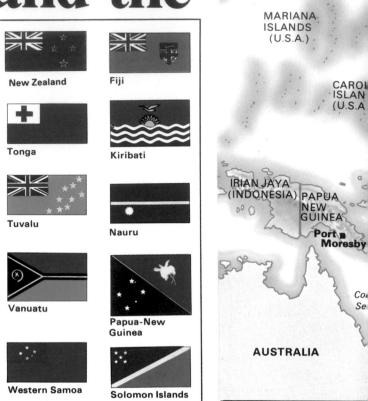

New Zealand Fiji

Tonga Kiribati

Tuvalu Nauru

Vanuatu Papua-New Guinea

Western Samoa Solomon Islands

MARIANA ISLANDS (U.S.A.)

CAROLINE ISLANDS (U.S.A.)

IRIAN JAYA (INDONESIA) PAPUA NEW GUINEA

Port Moresby

Coral Sea

AUSTRALIA

Above: An experienced sheep shearer can clip the wool from a sheep in less than thirty seconds.
Left: The island of Bora Bora in the Pacific is one of the Society Islands belonging to France. It was made by volcanoes and is mountainous. Other islands nearby are flat and made of coral. These islands are called *atolls*.

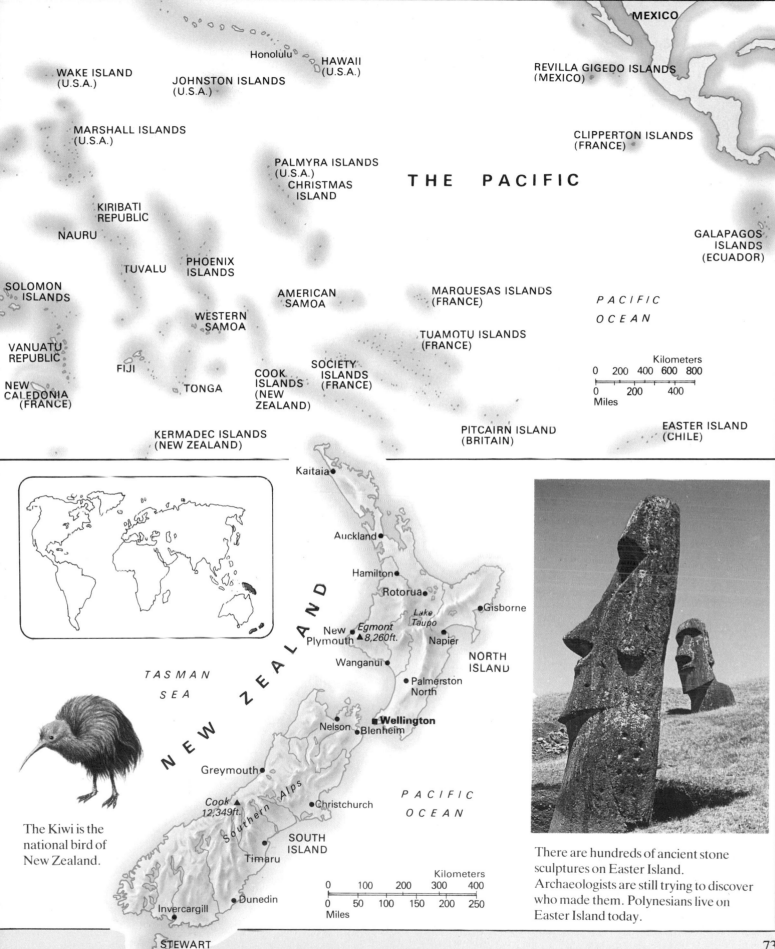

MEXICO

WAKE ISLAND
(U.S.A.)

Honolulu • HAWAII
(U.S.A.)

REVILLA GIGEDO ISLANDS
(MEXICO)

JOHNSTON ISLANDS
(U.S.A.)

MARSHALL ISLANDS
(U.S.A.)

CLIPPERTON ISLANDS
(FRANCE)

PALMYRA ISLANDS
(U.S.A.)
CHRISTMAS
ISLAND

THE   PACIFIC

KIRIBATI
REPUBLIC

GALAPAGOS
ISLANDS
(ECUADOR)

NAURU

PHOENIX
ISLANDS

TUVALU

SOLOMON
ISLANDS

MARQUESAS ISLANDS
(FRANCE)

PACIFIC

OCEAN

AMERICAN
SAMOA

WESTERN
SAMOA

TUAMOTU ISLANDS
(FRANCE)

VANUATU
REPUBLIC

FIJI

SOCIETY
ISLANDS
(FRANCE)

COOK
ISLANDS
(NEW
ZEALAND)

Kilometers

0   200 400 600 800

NEW
CALEDONIA
(FRANCE)

TONGA

0   200   400
Miles

KERMADEC ISLANDS
(NEW ZEALAND)

PITCAIRN ISLAND
(BRITAIN)

EASTER ISLAND
(CHILE)

Kaitaia •

Auckland •

Hamilton •

Rotorua •

Lake
Taupo

Gisborne

New *Egmont*
Plymouth ▲8,260ft.

Napier

TASMAN
SEA

Wanganui •

NORTH
ISLAND

N
E
W

Z
E
A
L
A
N
D

• Palmerston
North

■ **Wellington**

Nelson • • Blenheim

The Kiwi is the
national bird of
New Zealand.

Greymouth •

Southern Alps

Cook ▲
12,349ft.

• Christchurch

PACIFIC

OCEAN

SOUTH
ISLAND

Timaru •

Kilometers

0   100   200   300   400

0   50   100   150   200   250
Miles

Invercargill •

• Dunedin

STEWART
ISLAND

There are hundreds of ancient stone
sculptures on Easter Island.
Archaeologists are still trying to discover
who made them. Polynesians live on
Easter Island today.

The Polar Lands

PACIFIC OCEAN

ALASKA (U.S.A.)

BERING STRAIT

EAST SIBERIAN SEA

BEAUFORT SEA

NEW SIBERIAN ISLANDS

LAPTEV SEA

A Polar bear

BANKS ISLAND

CANADA

VICTORIA I.

ARCTIC OCEAN

QUEEN ELIZABETH ISLANDS

NORTH POLE

U.S.S.R.

ELLESMERE ISLAND

HUDSON BAY

Thule

FRANZ JOSEF LAND

BAFFIN ISLAND

BAFFIN BAY

NOVAYA ZEMLYA

SVALBARD (NORWAY)

BARENTS SEA

An Eskimo in a kayak

GREENLAND (DENMARK)

Godthaab

GREENLAND SEA

A Walrus

Murmansk

LAPLAND

Tromso

ARCTIC CIRCLE

NORWAY

SWEDEN

FINLAND

ATLANTIC OCEAN

Reykjavik ICELAND

The Arctic

The area around the North Pole is called the Arctic. Much of it consists of the icy Arctic Ocean. But there are islands, including Greenland. Parts of North America, Europe, and Asia also stretch beyond the *Arctic Circle*. The waters around the North Pole are frozen all the year round. But in other parts of the Arctic the snow melts during the short summer weeks and patches of moss, lichen, and bright flowers appear. These areas are the Arctic *tundra*. Eskimos are the only people living in the Arctic. Most live on the southwest coast of Greenland and are skilled hunters and fishermen.

The Antarctic

The continent of Antarctica covers almost 6 million square miles. It is larger than Europe and contains over 90 percent of the world's ice and snow. It is so bitterly cold in Antarctica that no one has ever lived there permanently. Whalers went there in the nineteenth century, but they never left the safety of their ships. Since 1911, when the South Pole was reached for the first time by Roald Amundsen, many scientists have been to the continent. They study the weather and the structure of the rocks buried in the ice. Research stations have been built there by a few countries, including the United States and the U.S.S.R.

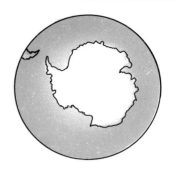

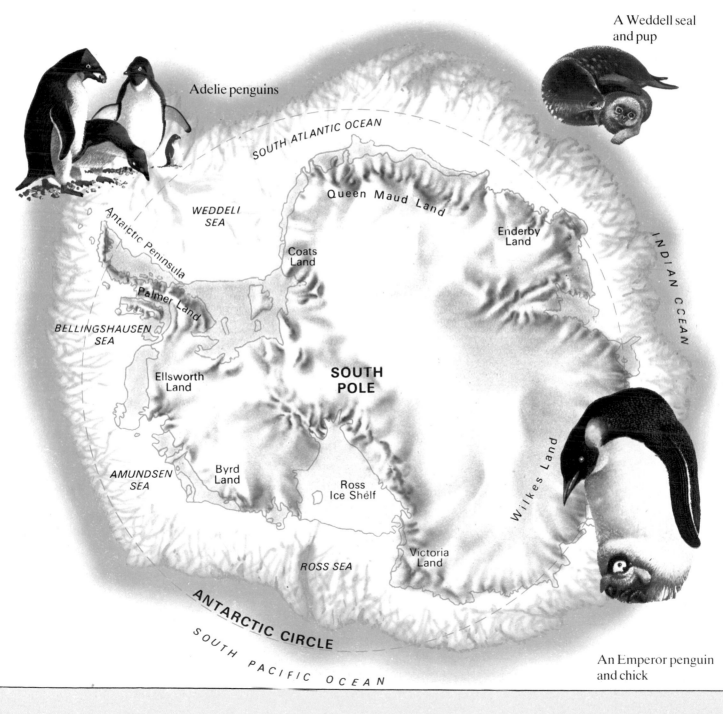

Adelie penguins

A Weddell seal and pup

SOUTH ATLANTIC OCEAN

Queen Maud Land

WEDDELL SEA

Enderby Land

Antarctic Peninsula

Coats Land

INDIAN OCEAN

Palmer Land

BELLINGSHAUSEN SEA

Ellsworth Land

SOUTH POLE

AMUNDSEN SEA

Byrd Land

Ross Ice Shelf

Wilkes Land

Victoria Land

ROSS SEA

ANTARCTIC CIRCLE

SOUTH PACIFIC OCEAN

An Emperor penguin and chick

Europe:
Facts and Figures

EUROPE

Country	Area (square miles)	Population	Capital	Official Language	Currency	Major Products
Albania	11,100	3,000,000	Tirana	Albanian	Lek	Oil, bitumen, metals (chrome, nickel, copper), tobacco, fruit, and vegetables
Andorra	175	32,700	Andorra la Vella	Catalan	French franc and Spanish peseta	Tourism, postage stamps
Austria	32,377	7,500,000	Vienna	German	Schilling	Food, iron and steel, textiles, paper products, machinery
Belgium	11,782	9,900,000	Brussels	Flemish, French	Belgian franc	Chemicals, vehicles, machinery, iron, steel
Bulgaria	42,826	8,900,000	Sofia	Bulgarian	Lev	Metals, machinery, textiles, tobacco, food
Czechoslovakia	49,377	15,500,000	Prague	Czech, Slovak	Koruna	Fuels, machinery, other manufactured goods, raw materials
Denmark	17,403	5,100,000	Copenhagen	Danish	Krone	Animals, meat, dairy produce, eggs, machinery, metals, and metal goods
Finland	130,129	4,900,000	Helsinki	Finnish, Swedish	Markka	Wood and wood pulp, paper, paperboard, machinery
France	211,223	55,000,000	Paris	French	French franc	Cars, electrical equipment, wine, cereals, textiles, leather goods, chemicals, iron, steel
Germany, East (German Democratic Republic—D.D.R.)	41,771	16,700,000	East Berlin	German	D.D.R. mark	Engineering goods, chemicals
Germany, West (Federal Republic of Germany)	95,983	61,000,000	Bonn	German	Deutschmark	Manufactured goods, chemicals, coke, consumer goods
Greece	50,948	10,100,000	Athens	Greek	Drachma	Manufactured goods, food, animals, wine, tobacco, chemicals
Hungary	35,922	10,800,000	Budapest	Hungarian	Forint	Transportation equipment, electrical goods, bauxite, aluminum, food, wine, pharmaceuticals
Iceland	39,771	200,000	Reykjavik	Icelandic	Krona	Fish products
Ireland, Republic of	27,138	3,600,000	Dublin	English, Irish	Irish pound (punt)	Meat and meat products, dairy products, beer, whiskey
Italy	116,322	57,400,000	Rome	Italian	Lira	Machinery, cars and trucks, iron and steel, textiles, footwear, plastics, fruit

Country	Area (square miles)	Population	Capital	Official Language	Currency	Major Products
Liechtenstein	60.6	26,000	Vaduz	German	Swiss franc	Cotton yarn and material, screws, bolts, needles
Luxembourg	999	400,000	Luxembourg	French, Luxemburgish (a German dialect)	Luxembourg franc	Iron and steel, chemicals, vehicles, machinery
Malta	122	400,000	Valletta	Maltese, English	Maltese pound	Food, manufactured goods, ship repairing, tourism
Monaco	0.7	25,000	Monaco	French	French franc	Tourism
Netherlands	15,771	14,500,000	Amsterdam; The Hague is the seat of government	Dutch	Guilder	Oil, chemicals, food and animals, machinery
Norway	125,191	4,200,000	Oslo	Norwegian	Krone	Animal products, paper, metals, metal products, fish, oil
Poland	120,734	37,300,000	Warsaw	Polish	Zloty	Lignite, coal, coke, iron and steel, ships, textiles, food
Portugal	35,556 (including Azores and Madeira)	10,400,000	Lisbon	Portuguese	Escudo	Textiles, timber, cork, machinery, chemicals, wine, sardines
Romania	91,706	22,800,000	Bucharest	Romanian	Leu	Food, machinery, minerals, metals, oil, natural gas, chemicals
San Marino	23.5	21,000	San Marino	Italian	Italian lira	Wine, cereals, cattle, tourism, postage stamps
Spain	194,912	38,600,000	Madrid	Spanish	Peseta	Manufactured goods, chemicals, textiles, leather goods, fish, wine, fruit and vegetables, olive oil
Sweden	173,245	8,300,000	Stockholm	Swedish	Swedish krona	Timber and timber products, machinery, metals and metal products, cars
Switzerland	15,943	6,500,000	Bern	French, German, Italian	Swiss franc	Tourism, machinery, chemicals and pharmaceuticals, watches, food, textiles
United Kingdom	94,535	56,400,000	London	English	Pound sterling	Manufactured goods, electrical and engineering products, transport equipment, textiles, chemicals, and plastics
U.S.S.R.	8,650,166	278,000,000	Moscow	Russian	Ruble	Iron, steel, chemicals, timber, paper, textiles (cotton), food, consumer goods
Vatican City State	0.17	1,000	Vatican City	Italian, Latin	Italian lira	
Yugoslavia	98,774	23,100,000	Belgrade	Serbo-Croat, Slovene, Macedonian	Dinar	Machinery, electrical goods, transportation equipment, chemicals

Asia:
Facts and Figures

ASIA

Country	Area (square miles)	Population	Capital	Official Language	Currency	Major Products
Afghanistan	250,018	14,700,000	Kabul	Pashtu, Dari	Afghani	Skins, cotton, natural gas, fruit
Bahrain	240	400,000	Manama	Arabic	Bahrain dinar	Oil
Bangladesh	55,602	101,500,000	Dhaka	Bengali	Taka	Jute, leather, hide and skins, tea
Bhutan	18,148	1,400,000	Thimphu	Dzongkha	Ngultrum	Rice, fruit, timber
Brunei	2,226	200,000	Bandar Seri Begawan	Malay	Brunei dollar	Oil
Burma	261,237	36,900,000	Rangoon	Burmese	Kyat	Teak, oil cake, rubber, jute
Cambodia (Kampuchea)	69,903	6,200,000	Phnom Penh	Khmer	Riel	Rice, rubber
China	3,705,677	1,042,000,000	Beijing (Peking)	Chinese (Mandarin)	Yuan	Industrial and agricultural products
Cyprus	3,572	700,000	Nicosia	Greek, Turkish	Cypriot pound	Fruit, vegetables, wine, manufactured goods, minerals
Hong Kong	404	5,500,000	Victoria	English, Chinese (Cantonese)	Hong Kong dollar	Light manufactured goods, textiles, electronics
India	1,269,438	762,200,000	New Delhi	Hindi, English	Indian rupee	Tea, industrial goods, jute, textiles
Indonesia	782,720	168,400,000	Jakarta	Bahasa (Indonesian)	Rupiah	Oil, palm products, rubber, coffee
Iran	636,343	45,100,000	Tehran	Persian (Farsi)	Rial	Oil, natural gas, cotton
Iraq	167,937	15,500,000	Baghdad	Arabic	Iraqi dinar	Oil, dates, wool, cotton
Israel	8,020	4,200,000	Jerusalem	Hebrew, Arabic	Shekel	Cut diamonds, chemicals, fruit, tobacco
Japan	143,761	120,800,000	Tokyo	Japanese	Yen	Optical equipment, ships, vehicles, machinery, electronic goods, chemicals, textiles
Jordan	37,740	3,600,000	Amman	Arabic	Jordanian dinar	Phosphates, fruit, vegetables

Country	Area (square miles)	Population	Capital	Official Language	Currency	Major Products
Korea, North	46,543	20,100,000	Pyongyang	Korean	Won	Iron and other metal ores
Korea, South	38,028	42,700,000	Seoul	Korean	Won	Textiles, manufactured goods, chemicals
Kuwait	6,880	1,900,000	Al Kuwait	Arabic	Kuwaiti dinar	Oil, chemicals
Laos	91,436	3,800,000	Vientiane	Lao	Kip	Timber, coffee
Lebanon	4,016	2,600,000	Beirut	Arabic	Lebanese pound	Precious metals, gemstones
Macao	6.2	300,000	Macao	Portuguese, Chinese	Pataca	Light manufactured goods
Malaysia	127,326	15,700,000	Kuala Lumpur	Malay	Ringgit	Rubber, tin, palm oil, timber
Maldive Islands	115	200,000	Malé	Divehi	Maldivian rupee	Fish, copra
Mongolia	604,294	1,900,000	Ulan Bator	Mongol	Tugrik	Cattle, horses, wool, hair
Nepal	54,366	17,000,000	Katmandu	Nepali	Nepalese rupee	Grains, hides, cattle, timber
Oman	82,036	1,200,000	Muscat	Arabic	Omani riyal	Oil, dates, limes, tobacco, frankincense
Pakistan	310,427	99,200,000	Islamabad	Urdu	Pakistani rupee	Cotton, carpets, leather, rice
Philippines	115,839	56,800,000	Manila	English, Pilipino	Piso	Sugar, timber, coconut products
Qatar	4,247	300,000	Doha	Arabic	Qatar riyal	Oil
Saudi Arabia	830,060	11,200,000	Riyadh	Arabic	Saudi riyal	Oil
Singapore	224	2,600,000	Singapore	Malay, Chinese, Tamil, English	Singapore dollar	Refined oil products, electronic goods, rubber
Sri Lanka	25,334	16,400,000	Colombo	Sinhala	Sri Lanka rupee	Tea, rubber, coconut products, industrial goods
Syria	71,504	10,600,000	Damascus	Arabic	Syrian pound	Cotton, oil, cereals, animals

Country	Area (square miles)	Population	Capital	Official Language	Currency	Major Products
Taiwan	13,886	19,200,000	Taipei	Chinese (Mandarin)	Taiwan dollar	Textiles, electrical goods, plastics, machinery, food
Thailand	198,471	52,700,000	Bangkok	Thai	Baht	Rice, tapioca, rubber, tin
Turkey	301,404	52,100,000	Ankara	Turkish	Turkish lira	Cotton, tobacco, nuts, fruit
United Arab Emirates	32,280	1,300,000	Abu Dhabi	Arabic	Dirham	Oil, natural gas
Vietnam	127,252	60,500,000	Hanoi	Vietnamese	Dong	Fish, coal, agricultural goods
Yemen, North (Arab Republic)	75,295	6,100,000	San'a	Arabic	Riyal	Cotton, coffee, hides, and skins
Yemen, South (P.D.R.)	128,569	2,100,000	Aden	Arabic	Dinar	Cotton, fish, refined oil

North America:
Facts and Figures

NORTH & CENTRAL AMERICA

Country	Area (square miles)	Population	Capital	Official Language	Currency	Major Products
Antigua and Barbuda	171	100,000	St. John's	English	East Caribbean dollar	Oil products
Bahamas	5,381	200,000	Nassau	English	Bahamian dollar	Oil products
Barbados	166	300,000	Bridgetown	English	East Caribbean dollar	Sugar, oil products, electrical goods, clothing
Belize	8,867	200,000	Belmopan	English, Spanish	Belize dollar	Sugar, bananas, citrus products, fish, clothing
Canada	3,852,085	25,400,000	Ottawa	English, French	Canadian dollar	Wheat, natural gas, oil, wood pulp, newsprint, iron ore, cars and parts, fish
Costa Rica	19,577	2,600,000	San Jose	Spanish	Colon	Coffee, bananas, manufactured goods
Cuba	44,221	10,100,000	Havana	Spanish	Peso	Sugar, tobacco

Country	Area (square miles)	Population	Capital	Official Language	Currency	Major Products
Dominica	290	100,000	Roseau	English	East Caribbean dollar	Citrus fruits, bananas
Dominican Republic	18,818	6,200,000	Santo Domingo	Spanish	Peso	Sugar, coffee
El Salvador	8,125	5,100,000	San Salvador	Spanish	Colon	Coffee, cotton
Grenada	133	100,000	St. George's	English	East Caribbean dollar	Cocoa, nutmeg, mace, bananas
Guatemala	42,045	8,000,000	Guatemala City	Spanish	Quetzal	Coffee, bananas, cotton, beef
Haiti	10,715	5,800,000	Port-au-Prince	French	Gourde	Coffee, bauxite, sugar
Honduras	43,281	4,400,000	Tegucigalpa	Spanish	Lempira	Coffee, bananas, timber, meat
Jamaica	4,244	2,300,000	Kingston	English	Jamaican dollar	Bauxite, alumina
Mexico	761,166	79,700,000	Mexico City	Spanish	Peso	Oil, coffee, cotton, sugar, manufactured goods
Nicaragua	50,197	3,000,000	Managua	Spanish	Cordoba	Cotton, coffee, meat, chemicals
Panama	29,211	2,000,000	Panama	Spanish	Balboa	Bananas, shrimps, sugar, oil products
St. Christopher (St. Kitts) and Nevis	101	40,000	Basseterre	English	East Caribbean dollar	Sugar
St. Lucia	238	100,000	Castries	English	East Caribbean dollar	Bananas, cocoa, citrus fruits, coconuts, tourism, manufactured goods
St. Vincent and the Grenadines	150	100,000	Kingstown	English	East Caribbean dollar	Bananas, arrowroot, coconuts
Trinidad and Tobago	1,981	1,200,000	Port of Spain	English	Trinidad dollar	Oil, asphalt, chemicals, sugar, fruit, cocoa, coffee
United States	3,615,385	238,900,000	Washington D.C.	English	U.S. dollar	Machinery, vehicles, aircraft and parts, iron and steel goods, coal, chemicals, cereals, soya beans, textiles, cotton

South America:
Facts and Figures

SOUTH AMERICA

Country	Area (square miles)	Population	Capital	Official Language	Currency	Major Products
Argentina	1,068,379	30,600,000	Buenos Aires	Spanish	Peso	Meat and meat products, tobacco, textiles, leather, machinery
Bolivia	422,265	6,200,000	La Paz (seat of government); Sucre (legal capital)	Spanish	Peso	Tin, oil, natural gas, cotton
Brazil	3,286,727	138,400,000	Brasilia	Portuguese	Cruzeiro	Machinery, vehicles, soya beans, coffee, cocoa
Chile	295,754	12,000,000	Santiago	Spanish	Peso	Wood pulp, paper, copper, timber, iron ore, nitrates
Colombia	439,769	29,400,000	Bogota	Spanish	Peso	Coffee, emeralds, sugar, oil, meat, skins, and hides
Ecuador	109,491	8,900,000	Quito	Spanish	Sucre	Oil, bananas, cocoa, coffee
French Guiana	35,138	76,000	Cayenne	French	French franc	Bauxite, shrimps, bananas
Guyana	82,632	800,000	Georgetown	English	Guyanese dollar	Sugar, rice, bauxite, alumina, timber
Paraguay	157,059	3,600,000	Asunción	Spanish	Guarani	Cotton, soya beans, tobacco, timber
Peru	496,261	19,500,000	Lima	Spanish	Sol	Metals, minerals (silver, lead, zinc, copper), fish
Surinam	63,042	400,000	Paramaribo	Dutch, English	Guilder	Bauxite, alumina, rice, citrus fruit
Uruguay	68,042	3,000,000	Montevideo	Spanish	Peso	Meat, wool, hides, and skins
Venezuela	352,170	17,300,000	Caracas	Spanish	Bolivar	Oil, iron, cocoa, coffee

Africa:
Facts and Figures

AFRICA

Country	Area (square miles)	Population	Capital	Official Language	Currency	Major Products
Algeria	919,662	22,200,000	Algiers	Arabic	Algerian dinar	Natural gas, oil
Angola	481,389	7,900,000	Luanda	Portuguese	Kwanza	Coffee, diamonds, oil
Benin	43,487	4,000,000	Porto Novo	French	Franc C.F.A.	Cocoa, cotton
Botswana	231,822	1,100,000	Gaborone	English, Setswana	Pula	Copper, diamonds, meat
Burkina Faso	105,877	6,900,000	Ouagadougou	French	Franc C.F.A.	Livestock, groundnuts, cotton
Burundi	10,748	4,600,000	Bujumbura	French, Kirundi	Burundi franc	Coffee
Cameroon	183,583	9,700,000	Yaounde	English, French	Franc C.F.A.	Cocoa, coffee, oil
Cape Verde Islands	1,557	300,000	Praia	Portuguese	Escudo	Bananas, fish
Central African Republic	240,553	2,700,000	Bangui	French	Franc C.F.A.	Coffee, diamonds, timber
Chad	495,791	5,200,000	N'Djamena	French	Franc C.F.A.	Cotton, cattle, meat
Comoros	838	500,000	Moroni	French	Franc C.F.A.	Spices
Congo	132,057	1,700,000	Brazzaville	French	Franc C.F.A.	Oil, timber
Djibouti	8,495	300,000	Djibouti	French	Djibouti franc	Cattle, hides, and skins
Egypt	386,690	48,300,000	Cairo	Arabic	Egyptian pound	Cotton, oil, textiles
Equatorial Guinea	10,831	300,000	Malabo	Spanish	Ekuele	Cocoa, coffee, timber
Ethiopia	471,812	36,000,000	Addis Ababa	Amharic	Ethiopian dollar	Coffee, hides, and skins

Country	Area (square miles)	Population	Capital	Official Language	Currency	Major Products
Gabon	103,354	1,000,000	Libreville	French	Franc C.F.A.	Manganese, oil
Gambia	4,361	800,000	Banjul	English	Dalasi	Groundnuts
Ghana	92,106	14,300,000	Accra	English	Cedi	Cocoa, gold, timber
Guinea	94,971	6,100,000	Conakry	French	Syli	Alumina, bauxite
Guinea-Bissau	13,949	900,000	Bissau	Portuguese	Escudo	Fish, groundnuts
Ivory Coast	124,513	10,100,000	Abidjan	French	Franc C.F.A.	Cocoa, coffee, timber
Kenya	224,977	20,200,000	Nairobi	English, Swahili	Kenya shilling	Coffee, tea, hides
Lesotho	11,721	1,500,000	Maseru	English, Sesotho	Loti	Wool, mohair
Liberia	43,003	2,200,000	Monrovia	English	Liberian dollar	Iron ore, rubber
Libya	679,412	4,000,000	Tripoli	Arabic	Libyan dinar	Oil
Madagascar	226,674	10,000,000	Antananarivo	French, Malagasy	Malgache franc	Coffee, spices, vanilla
Malawi	45,750	7,100,000	Lilongwe	English, Chichewa	Kwacha	Tobacco, tea
Mali	478,801	7,700,000	Bamako	French	Mali franc	Groundnuts, cotton
Mauritania	397,984	1,900,000	Nouakchott	Arabic, French	Ouguiya	Iron ore, copper
Mauritius	805	1,000,000	Port Louis	English	Rupee	Sugar, tea, tobacco
Morocco	172,426	24,300,000	Rabat	Arabic	Dirham	Phosphates, fruit
Mozambique	302,352	13,900,000	Maputo	Portuguese	Metical	Sugar, fruit, vegetables
Namibia	318,284	1,100,000	Windhoek	Afrikaans, English	Rand	Minerals, diamonds, fish

Country	Area (square miles)	Population	Capital	Official Language	Currency	Major Products
Niger	489,227	6,500,000	Niamey	French	Franc C.F.A.	Groundnuts, livestock, uranium
Nigeria	356,695	91,200,000	Lagos	English	Naira	Oil, palm kernels, cocoa
Rwanda	10,170	6,300,000	Kigali	French, Kinyarwanda	Rwanda franc	Coffee
Sao Tome and Principe	373	100,000	Sao Tomé	Portuguese	Dobra	Cocoa
Senegal	75,756	6,700,000	Dakar	French	Franc C.F.A.	Groundnuts, phosphates
Seychelles	108	100,000	Victoria	English, French	Rupee	Copra, fish, spices
Sierra Leone	27,701	3,600,000	Freetown	English	Leone	Diamonds, iron ore
Somali Republic	246,219	6,500,000	Mogadishu	Somali	Somali shilling	Livestock
South Africa	471,479	32,500,000	Pretoria (seat of government); Cape Town (legal capital)	Afrikaans, English	Rand	Gold, diamonds, fruit, vegetables
Sudan	967,570	21,800,000	Khartoum	Arabic	Sudanese pound	Cotton, groundnuts
Swaziland	6,704	600,000	Mbabane	English	Lilangeni	Sugar, wood pulp, asbestos, fruit
Tanzania	364,927	21,700,000	Dodoma	English, Swahili	Tanzanian shilling	Coffee, cotton, sisal, spices
Togo	21,623	3,000,000	Lomé	French	Franc C.F.A.	Phosphates, cocoa, coffee
Tunisia	63,175	7,200,000	Tunis	Arabic	Tunisian dinar	Phosphates, olive oil, oil
Uganda	91,141	14,700,000	Kampala	English	Ugandan shilling	Coffee, cotton
Zaire	905,633	33,100,000	Kinshasa	French	Zaire	Coffee, cobalt, copper
Zambia	290,607	6,800,000	Lusaka	English	Kwacha	Copper
Zimbabwe	150,815	8,600,000	Harare	English	Zimbabwe dollar	Tobacco

Oceania:
Facts and Figures

THE PACIFIC

Country	Area (square miles)	Population	Capital	Official Language	Currency	Major Products
Australia	2,968,125	15,800,000	Canberra	English	Australian dollar	Cereals, meat, sugar, honey, fruit, metals and mineral ores, wool
Fiji	7,056	700,000	Suva	English, Fijian	Fiji dollar	Sugar, coconut oil
Kiribati	359	60,000	Tarawa	English, Gilbertese	Australian dollar	Copra, phosphates, fish
Nauru	8.1	8,000	Nauru	English, Nauruan	Australian dollar	Phosphates
New Zealand	103,744	3,400,000	Wellington	English	New Zealand dollar	Meat, dairy products, wool, fruit
Papua New Guinea	178,273	3,300,000	Port Moresby	English	Kina	Copra, cocoa, coffee, copper
Solomon Islands	10,984	300,000	Honiara	English	Solomon Islands dollar	Timber, fish, copra, palm oil
Tonga	270	100,000	Nuku'alofa	English	Pa'anga	Copra, bananas
Tuvalu	9.7	8,000	Fongafale	English, Tuvalu	Australian dollar	Copra
Vanuatu	5,700	100,000	Port Vila	Bislama, English, French	Vatu	Copra, fish
Western Samoa	1,097	200,000	Apia	English, Samoan	Tala	Copra, cocoa, bananas

General Index

Map Index

PHOTOGRAPHIC ACKNOWLEDGMENTS

The publishers wish to thank ZEFA for supplying the photographs for the cover and most of the photographs inside the book.

Additional photographs were supplied by J. Allan Cash (p. 9 *right*), Royal Netherlands Embassy (p. 17), British Tourist Board (p. 18 *top*), Renault (p. 20 *top right*), Italian Tourist Office (p. 28 *top*), Hungarian Tourist Office (p. 30 *bottom*), Greek Tourist Office (p. 33 *top*), Novosti (p. 34 *left*), Dave Collins (p. 38 *top right*), Sharp Electronics (p. 42 *top*), Thailand Tourist Board (p. 44 *top left*), New Jersey Travel and Tourism (p. 50 *right*), Rowntrees (p. 64 *right*), Satour (p. 68 *left* and *bottom*), Australian News and Information Bureau (p. 70 *left* and *top*), New Zealand Tourist Office (p. 72 *right*).